GROWING A
MEDICAL
PRACTICE

GROWING A
MEDICAL
PRACTICE

FROM FRUSTRATION TO A HIGH
PERFORMANCE BUSINESS

SARAH BARTHOLOMEUSZ

Surrounded by medical business and being a business owner I was able to immediately identify with the points that Sarah has identified as shortfalls in the medical business industry. This book provides strategies and motivation for realising the dreams of owning a successful medical practice in a practical manner. Not only will this book improve the life quality of business health professionals but also the care provided to the patients of those practices. It is the first of its kind written with insight and knowledge usually only seen in the inner circles of medical services.

Dr April Armstrong, General Practice Owner and Founder & Director, Business for Doctors Pty Ltd, Western Australia

The best part of this book is the whole book! I think it is essential reading for all doctors who want to set up and run a medical practice. The book makes you think about business and legal principles in running your practice. It gives you guidance from the conception stage of a medical clinic to succession planning, in great detail. The book is well organised and easy to read. There is a lot of information on issues such as risk management, contracts, leases, marketing, practice structure, partnerships and much more.

Dr Umair Masood, Neal Street Medical Clinic, Victoria

There are things you need to know when running a medical business but you don't always know what they are. This book will tell you.

Dr Matthew Barber, Gladstone Road Medical Centre, Queensland

Love the very pertinent quotations from various sources at the start of each chapter. Very relevant for doctors who as Sarah highlights are not your usual business people.

General Practitioner, Henley Beach, South Australia

Sarah delivers a vast array of high-quality information that is pertinent to practitioners embarking on their careers and also those wanting to review their current practice. Well written, her narrative provides comprehensive and practical advice in an insightful manner. This book is an excellent tool to assist the growth of any medical practice.

Corrine Allison, General Manager, AllCo Innovation, South Australia

A comprehensive book explaining all the bits of medical practice that doctors receive no training in.

Dr Shauna Watts, General Practitioner, New South Wales

It is good to be reminded that medical practices and related businesses face the same obligations, challenges and pitfalls as other businesses. Perhaps the ways in which these issues manifest are slightly different, but the risks remain and can be mitigated. This book helps to crystallise thinking about the issues involved.

Dr Chris Alderman, Australian Medication Safety Services, South Australia

In a previous role I managed a large medical practice in Melbourne. It would have been good to share this book with the practice principals. What I explained in various board meetings would have been answered by this book. It is food for thought, and if you are a doctor contemplating making the leap to being a practice owner, then this book should be one of your guides.

David Frost, Chief Financial Officer, Dementia Australia, Victoria

ABOUT THE AUTHOR

Sarah Bartholomeusz is the Principal of award-winning law firm You Legal – a new category of law firm providing commercial legal services to Australian doctors. In short, they are lawyers who take care of doctors. (And Sarah's clients even call her the 'Goddess of Governance'.)

In addition to her BA and LL.B from the University of Adelaide, Sarah has a Graduate Diploma of Applied Corporate Governance from the Governance Institute of Australia Ltd, of which she is a Fellow. Sarah is also a Graduate of the Australian Institute of Directors Company Director's Course and a Member of the Law Society of South Australia.

Sarah's insight into the way legal services are transforming was recognised in 2015 when she won the South Australian Telstra Business Women's Award in the Start-Up category. She was also awarded the Lawyers Weekly Women in Law Awards 'Thought Leader of the Year Award' for 2016.

Sarah's first book, *How to Avoid a Fall from Grace: Legal Lessons for Directors*, was ranked as a #1 best seller on Amazon after its release in 2015. Sarah's second book, *Kingpin: Legal Lessons from the Underworld*, explores crucial legal lessons mainstream businesses can learn from the inherently risky and volatile underworld inhabited by the most infamous 'kingpins' in history. She also regularly writes for *The Huffington Post* and *CEO Magazine*.

You Legal has appeared on *Sky News*, Channel 10's morning show *Studio 10*, in the *Weekend Australian*, *CEO Magazine*, Adelaide's *The Advertiser*, and websites Law Management Hub, Short Press, Business News Australia, Legal Practice Intelligence, Australasian Lawyer and Dynamic Business.

In addition to her business and publishing, Sarah is the Chair of the Catalyst Foundation Inc., a charitable and inclusive organisation providing information and support for older, vulnerable people and those with disability. Catalyst Foundation's vision is that these people will achieve better opportunities through self-advocacy, services and support to live their lives as they choose. She serves on the South Australian Government's Education Standards Board, and is also a mentor for the University of Adelaide's ThincLab.

Sarah loves to hear from readers. To connect via You Legal:

* email: sarah@youlegal.com.au
* call: 1300 870 661

For more background information, please visit www.youlegal.com.au.

First published in 2018 by Sarah Bartholomeusz

A catalogue entry for this book is available from the National Library of Australia.

ISBN: 978-1-925648-75-1

Project management and text design by Michael Hanrahan Publishing
Cover design by Peter Reardon

Disclaimer
The material in this publication is of the nature of general comment only, and does not represent professional advice. It is not intended to provide specific guidance for particular circumstances and it should not be relied on as the basis for any decision to take action or not take action on any matter which it covers. Readers should obtain professional advice where appropriate, before making any such decision. To the maximum extent permitted by law, the author and publisher disclaim all responsibility and liability to any person, arising directly or indirectly from any person taking or not taking action based on the information in this publication.

CONTENTS

Introduction   1

Legal disclaimer   8

PART I: DEPRESSION, ANXIETY AND STRESS SCALE FOR YOUR BUSINESS

1   Business owner mindset versus doctor mindset   11

2   Continuing as the high achiever   17

PART II: A FLU SHOT FOR YOUR BUSINESS

3   How medical professionals think about risk   23

4   Contracts and insurance   39

5   Operations manuals and disclaimers   49

6   Privacy policies and data protection   55

PART III: X-RAY FOR YOUR BUSINESS: SEARCHING FOR HIDDEN FRACTURES

7   What does a healthy medical business look like?   69

8   Business triage: Ready for growth and what can potentially kill a business?   73

9   Practice structure – let's run some tests   81

10   Documenting what has been agreed: Shareholders' agreements   93

11   Your intellectual property is a business asset   99

PART IV: OPERATIONS DON'T JUST HAPPEN IN THEATRE

12 Lease, licence or landlord: Legal lessons in bricks and mortar   109

13 Essential elements of an employee contract   121

14 Building a team   125

15 Growing your team   135

16 Myth busting: Contractor doctors   141

17 Managing a patient grievance and understanding competition law   147

PART V: THE BUSINESS MEDICAL

18 Marketing your medical business   157

19 The fear of disruption is irrational   161

20 Determining the financial value and compliance requirements of your practice   165

21 Personal succession planning   171

Conclusion   177

Appendix A: Sample operations manual: Table of contents   179

Appendix B: Shareholders' agreement checklist   183

Appendix C: Record-keeping requirements for all business areas   189

INTRODUCTION

It is not the strongest of the species that survives, nor the most intelligent. It is the one most responsive to change.

Commonly accepted summary of the central idea outlined in Charles Darwin's On the Origin of Species

How does the business world frustrate the practice of medicine? Some of the smartest doctors in the operating room feel powerless in the boardroom or, on a smaller scale, when running a small business.

Medical schools teach the mechanics of being a great doctor, while hospital and specialist training help medical professionals find their niche. They go on to work harder and harder, devoting their time to improving your skills within a specialty. Perhaps you can relate to this. You're now at the stage of running your own business, but this can pose a plethora of problems seemingly unrelated to the profession you studied your whole life.

Perhaps you feel as if, when you chose a specialty long ago, you jumped onto a train and trusted it would take you where you wanted to go. You trusted that the people on the train would instruct you along the way. But now that you've reached your destination – owning your own practice – you may not feel the excitement or satisfaction you imagined you would feel upon disembarking from the train.

Googling the phrase 'how to run a medical business' returns 5.5 million related results. So, while plenty of advice is available on how to run and grow a business, there is also a definitive glut of information for operating a medical practice – how do you know where to start?

This book is not simply a book about the best practices you can use when legally running a business. While it does consider issues like reviewing your business structure, employment law, intellectual property, privacy compliance and contracts, it also considers modern leadership techniques along with providing a glimpse into the future with some ideas about how to examine your medical practice for the best possible outcomes – by thinking about technology and innovation in your business, for example. Before launching into the 'guts' of the book, let me tell you a bit about me and how I ended up wanting to help doctors in their practices.

HOW LOSING MY CORPORATE JOB TRANSFORMED MY LIFE

I love sharing my story because I have always found it fascinating how people are inspired by the great ideas and reasons behind starting businesses. Some start a business because they see a problem they would like to solve, others have an epiphany while washing the dishes after dinner, and still others classify themselves as accidental entrepreneurs who never saw their business success coming. I believe I fall somewhere in the middle of those three. Back in 2013, when I first started my own firm, there was just one lawyer – me – and one foundation client.

A few months earlier, I was standing on the 34th floor of an office building overlooking Sydney Harbour. I was holding a multi-million-dollar cheque, but it wasn't mine; my role in the company I worked for was to sell one of my company's non-core assets, and this cheque was the final result. As I handed the cheque over, I realised two things: I was now out of a job, and I needed to find a new way to work.

At the time, I was seven months pregnant with my second child, and my father had just been diagnosed with cancer. It wasn't an ideal time to be out of work, but it was the push I needed to create a workplace that would address my need for work–life balance and to find solutions to the flaws I encountered in the corporate law model. One major flaw in the traditional corporate workplace was that it meant working extremely long hours. At any given time, one in three lawyers working in a traditional firm is suffering from stress, high anxiety or depression. At the same time, their clients don't always feel they have received good value for the legal fees paid. So I set out to create a different sort of company.

Fast-forward to August 2017, and I was in Fiji presenting for a group of doctors. As part of my presentation, I described, with some passion, why I started You Legal, and why I wanted it to be different from other commercial law firms. As I explained my issues with the legal profession to the conference room of doctors, their heads began to nod wildly. It was immediately apparent that the medical profession has many similar pitfalls.

I explained the complaints that clients of lawyers regularly make – including the lack of communication they feel they receive from lawyers about their matters, and the expense and the inefficiencies they perceive in the traditional model. I explained that these complaints were issues I hoped to address with my new You Legal model, as I worked to provide clear communication, find efficiencies in practice and provide value for legal services. The conference attendees noted that they received similar complaints about the medical profession from patients.

I explained to the conference attendees that I kept these problems foremost in my mind when I founded the business I envisioned as the law firm of the future: a law firm that clients loved to work with and lawyers loved to work for. The added bonus, at least in the initial stages of the business, was that I could work from home.

The core of my inspiration was that I did not want to just survive this period of stress and uncertainty; I wanted to thrive because of it. I saw an opportunity, and I threw myself at it with full force. I had taken note of how technology could drive efficiency and reduce costs. So, from the very beginning, we functioned as a firm that provided legal services clients could access from wherever and whenever they wanted.

Without having the overhead of a bricks-and-mortar practice, time and money were freed up to hire qualified staff across a huge range of specialties. This futuristic model proved to be successful. I believe that an enormous part of our success comes from having built a strong team of dreamers and doers who share and contribute to the firm's vision and values.

People love to engage with an idea and passion, and an example of this comes from another travel story. During a family trip home from a friend's wedding in Europe, we stopped over in Dubai. It was 40°C at 11 pm, but everyone in the airport was dressed for autumn in coats and scarves. We were all tired, hot and listless. Suddenly, on a quiet bus transporting travellers between terminals, a voice started singing, 'If you're happy and you know it'. It was my son, Alex, three years old, bored and looking for a way to break the tedium. Within a few moments, someone else joined in, and the two of them were singing and clapping together. Then another joined, and another. By the time he reached the end of the song, the whole bus was singing and clapping along. The mood was transformed.

In a very similar way, my firm found its niche for both lawyers and clients. Now operating across Australia as a legal team of more than 20 experts from three different countries, we have grown from one person singing to a whole busload of people singing and clapping along.

PEOPLE WHO HELP PEOPLE

Both during and after the conference in Fiji, my team was working on a mergers and acquisitions deal, which involved selling one of our client businesses for, what I thought was a staggering, $500 million AUD (yes, half a *billion* dollars). Despite the benefits of my new business model, the team was working crazy hours on this deal for months and months on end. Once the deal completed, I was sitting in a coffee shop with one of my mentors and, while drinking my almond-milk flat white, I told her the deal was finally complete. She was so excited for me and said, 'That is such an incredible achievement. You should be celebrating all day and all night.' But I wasn't. I was deflated. I was well and truly spent.

This conversation initiated a massive wave of self-reflection. When I'd set up my business four years previously, the business values I'd put in place were Unstoppable, Fresh, Love and Thoughtful. In the aftermath of completing the deal, I wondered whether these values were still as meaningful today as they were then. I realised spending all our time working with corporate clients no longer served You Legal or its values. Reviewing our existing clients and those we had served in the past four years, I found the clients who gave me energy to work with were those who were in the business of helping people.

I think it's often forgotten that what lawyers do is help people. The media and some dinner conversations certainly seem to focus on the devious nature of lawyers, but, at the core of their work, lawyers exist to assist others. For the same reason, many legal professionals experience mental health problems.

The client review resulted in an epiphany – I wanted my business to only act for people who help people. And from this, I became even more specific. We would be 'the lawyers who take care of doctors'. The conference in Fiji was a major contributor to this shift, but so was my family background.

I come from a medical family. Two of my uncles and one cousin are orthopaedic surgeons. I have a cousin who is a general surgeon, and another cousin graduated from med school just a few years ago. Another cousin is a nurse, and I have additional uncles and cousins working in allied health.

At holiday gatherings, I've also heard many stories about family members in the medical industry receiving professional services so dubious that the anecdotes made my toes curl up inside my shoes. One Christmas, my uncle (who is a surgeon) arrived for the holidays declaring he had just bought shares in a fish farm in New South Wales. At the time, he lived in South Australia, so the investment did not make much sense. As I understand it, my uncle is still the owner of this investment, and has been unable to sell down his position. As a result of stories such as these, I have always had a great personal interest in protecting my relatives' wealth and business interests.

WHO SHOULD READ THIS BOOK

Every man has a specific skill, whether it is discovered or
not, that more readily and naturally comes to him than
it would to another, and his own should be sought and
polished. He excels best in his niche – originality loses
its authenticity in one's efforts to obtain originality.

Criss Jami, Salomé: In Every Inch In Every Mile

I've no doubt you are amazing at what you do and super compliance-
focused. You've also picked up this book, however, so chances are you
don't quite know where to start with making your practice legally
compliant – and this makes your life a living nightmare. You're unsure
what impact potentially having a practice that's not legally compliant
actually has, and you're unaware of the issues that could potentially kill
your business.

You have built your practice around your own skills. Your accountant
may tell you that your practice is operating well, and to keep doing what
you're doing, but even so, you may feel uncomfortable about certain
aspects of your business. You may feel like working harder all the time is
not getting you to the level of security you want, or where you know the
business could be. This is where this book comes in. Following the steps
in it can help you to stop worrying about your medical business and
focus on your 'zone of genius' – that is, the place where you know you
make the biggest difference to the largest number of people.

SO WHERE SHOULD WE START?

We start in this zone of genius. As you read this book, I will be asking
you to do something you may not have been asked to do during your
medical training. I will ask you to concentrate on self-awareness to
cultivate yourself as the foundation of your business. This may seem
obvious to you, but sometimes practices are initiated by focusing on
the skills you have acquired, rather than on the authentic version of

yourself. If you build your medical business in complete alignment with who you are and what you are naturally talented at and love doing, while simultaneously cultivating the lifestyle that you desire, you will be boarding a train on tracks destined to achieve the life that you want.

So what is a 'zone of genius'? A zone of genius is based on your raw talents, strengths and personality type. Once you've found this zone, the next step is to assemble a team of talent that complements it. By doing this, you can get into 'the flow' – that special place where work feels like play, comes more easily, and doesn't leave you or your employees feeling drained at the end of each day. When you exist and work in this zone, you discover your own style of creativity, along with the ways in which you inspire yourself and others, and the activities that give you limitless amounts of energy. As a result, you are a better entrepreneur and all-around happier doctor and person.

Regardless of what advice you seek and adopt to build your practice, one sure-fire strategy is embodied in the Greek aphorism, 'temet nosce', or 'know thyself'. Self-awareness is a winning strategy promoted throughout this book. So let's get started.

LEGAL DISCLAIMER

Would you have been disappointed if this book did not include a legal disclaimer? I bet you would have. Well, here it is. This book is an overview of the law at a specific point in time and is very general in nature. It should not be relied on as a substitute for legal advice. In addition, with the law in this area changing regularly, this book is unlikely to remain a comprehensive guide for long. I hope, though, that it can be used as a guide to mitigate your personal risk and highlight some items worthy of consideration and discussion in the boardroom. Please feel free to contact You Legal regarding anything in this book, and we may be able to assist you.

In addition, I am not a tax lawyer. Tax law is a very specialised area of the law, and I do not address Australian (or any other country's) tax laws in any detail in this book. Although I talk about legally structuring your practice, I make numerous references to obtaining specific tax advice not covered in this book. I am also going to remind you, several times, of the importance of consulting a tax professional/lawyer.

PART I

DEPRESSION, ANXIETY AND STRESS SCALE FOR YOUR BUSINESS

Life is amazing, and then it's awful, and then it's amazing again, and in between the amazing and the awful it's ordinary, mundane and routine. Breathe in the amazing, hold on through the awful, and relax and exhale through the ordinary. That's just living. Heartbreaking, soul healing, amazing, awful, ordinary, life, and its breathtakingly beautiful.

LR Knost

Setting up your own practice may not have turned out quite as you expected. When you first set up your practice, you were getting paid well for the work you loved, and you worked hard to bring in patients and hone the services you wanted to provide. Your friends and family thought you were living the dream.

As a very high achiever – super, crazy high achiever by society's standards – you may not always feel as satisfied in your work as others perceive you to be. You may sometimes feel as though you're struggling to close a persistent gap between where you are and where you want to be. Maybe you have seen others in your profession take time off, build a legacy, and lead teams of talented people. If you are reading this book, those are things you want – and the tips and tools provided here can help you transform your business to achieve those goals.

Running your own business – and feeling like you're not quite achieving everything you'd hoped, no matter how hard you work – can cause anxiety, stress and even depression. So before we get to the mechanics of running your medical business, the chapters in the first part of this book look at your mindset, and how to adopt a business mindset that's positive and high achieving. Let's start with what's so bad about the doctor's mindset – the topic of chapter 1.

1 BUSINESS OWNER MINDSET VERSUS DOCTOR MINDSET

The body achieves what the mind believes.

Anonymous

When your goals do not match your mindset in business, the actions you take to move forward may not actually close the gap between your present reality and your intended destination. In other words, when your attitude is not in synch with your goals, realising the goals you have will be much more difficult and take longer.

As already mentioned, this mismatch for medical professionals commonly occurs because the training you're offered at medical school and after graduation does not teach a business owner mindset. The doctor's mindset you have cultivated is incongruent with the mentality of a business owner. In the next chapter, I cover preparing your positive mindset for achieving your goals, while this chapter focuses on how the doctor's mindset might be holding you back. But first, let's remember how it all started.

YOUR GOALS WHEN YOU STARTED YOUR BUSINESS VERSUS NOW

When you started your practice and envisioned making a living doing the work you'd trained for many years to do and loved doing, you didn't know any different. You may not have, at that point, had a vision for something bigger. You just wanted to love your work and not have someone else telling you what to do.

You have done a fantastic job getting to where you are – operating your own medical practice is something very few people on the planet are able to do. Absolutely nothing is wrong with continuing to do what you are doing. Nothing is 'less than' about doing great work every day and exploring your craft. If that sounds exactly like what you want, own it. And, at the same time, realise that the goals you have need to match that mindset. If you want to create something bigger than yourself, however, something is going to have to shift.

When you first started your practice, your goals may have been to replace the income from your previous role, acquire a steady stream of patients and make a difference in the health of those patients. Those are great goals. However, for many practitioners, achieving those goals creates the persistent feeling that they are always struggling to get further ahead. You may have found you could increase your income, treat more patients and have a positive impact on those patients' health but, on the flipside, you may have also found you have not been able to take a break or raise revenue past a point that compensates you for the value of your time.

Many of these problems occur because you are working towards business owner's goals with a doctor's mindset. This can create an incredibly frustrating situation. Each mindset has a set of goals associated with it and, while there's significant wiggle room in each, there's very little overlap. The following sections look at some of the main differences between a doctor and a business mindset.

WORKING *IN* INSTEAD OF *ON* YOUR BUSINESS

If your priority is digging in and doing the work, owning a practice is a great way to do this. Working with patients is hugely important, personally rewarding – and also fun – and will always be an important part of your schedule. Looking at the tasks that must be completed, however, and delegating these to others or investigating what can be automated can help you focus on the bigger picture. You need time to think about business development, which involves reviewing 'outside the box' alternative revenue streams and exploring ways to leverage other people to create additional value for your patients.

When your priority is on doing *all* the work, you don't have time to review options for restructuring your practice's model, examine new revenue streams, or build teams. Doing all the work is just one business model, and a perfectly acceptable way of operating your practice. However, you need to check your goals and make sure that your goals are aligned with doing all the work yourself.

FOCUSING ON THE 'WHAT' INSTEAD OF THE 'WHO'

If your priority is figuring out 'what' you need to do instead of 'who' can do it for you, you're not in business owner mode. When an idea or opportunity comes your way, if your first thought is 'I wonder what I need to do to get better at so I can take advantage of that', that's your doctor's mindset talking.

Acknowledging that others can not only do the task, but also do it better than you can be a hard transition in perspective. When you're accustomed to being the smartest person in the room, accepting that your practice won't ever be as good as it could be if you don't involve others can be very difficult. Once you acknowledge the advantages of delegating tasks, however, you have shifted from doctor to business owner mindset.

Like most doctors, you are probably a perfectionist. To become more like a business owner, you can change your thinking to focus on 'who' when there's something new you want to explore in the practice. As your team grows, the shift in thinking might even become, Who is better at this than I am? Who already knows how to do this? Who has already done this before? Whose personal values would allow me to expand the scope of my business beyond my own?

Employing people isn't just about getting help. Employing people is the best way to expand beyond your own limitations of knowledge, values and capacity. This means employing people doesn't just free up your time so you can do more; it changes the very nature of the way your practice can deliver value. (In chapters 14 and 15, I cover building and growing your team in much more detail.)

The doctor mindset may guide you to employing people who can help you do more of the same kind of work you already do, while reclaiming a little sanity. Business owners know that employing people increases the amount of value (and, therefore, most often revenue) their businesses (or, in our case, practices) create.

FOCUSING ON YOUR SALARY INSTEAD OF PROFIT

If you'd like to do great work for a great salary, working as a doctor and not thinking too much about building your practice could be the way to go. Perhaps you have already heard about the time-for-money trap, but I'm not talking about just that.

Let's first clarify exactly what the time-for-money trap is. It is the very common belief that working means trading time for money. This idea starts early in our lives – when we are told by our parents, grandparents, aunts and uncles that if we work in a stable job for 40 to 50 hours a week, getting paid for our time, we will have enough money to retire at 60 or 65. Professionals find breaking out of this understanding particularly hard; however, it is one of society's biggest hoaxes. Time is our most important commodity, and all of the money in the world cannot compensate us for it.

When you are in the mindset of trading time for money, your income will always be limited. Why? Well, each day only has 24 hours to devote to the pursuit of money. Most people need eight or so hours for sleep, additional time to commute to and from work, and at least four hours to cook, eat, and spend time with family and friends. As a medical professional you're likely used to carving out slightly less time for eating, sleeping and socialising, but in general most people are left with 10 to 12 hours they can trade for income. That is all. The fact is that no matter how much you charge per hour for your time – even if it is $1000 or $10,000 – time is always the limiting factor.

If you want a great salary, assets that increase in value and a healthy share of profit from a great business, you need to shift to the business owner mindset. This is because the doctor mindset can exclude a tremendously important part of the business-building equation: profit.

To become profitable, you must examine the true value your practice is creating, which is not often visible on the surface. If you can work out how to scale to a certain point, you can create additional efficiency in the way the value is delivered, and you can look for ways to innovate on the way the value is traditionally created. Creating profit is a process of optimising effectiveness and efficiency.

So what does it mean to 'scale'? Scale is a term that business people use often and can have differing meanings, depending on the context. In the context of this book, I mean businesses that can scale or increase their operations can create operating leverage for the owner. Businesses that can scale can grow revenue with minimal or no increase in operating costs (for example, administrative costs). Scalability is a characteristic of a system, model or function that can perform under an increased or expanding workload.

Examine the services and products you're offering now. How much of the revenue you're creating from them is actually profit? How much just pays for your time?

When you've been focused on paying yourself for so long – and no doubt have an incredible work ethic – breaking into profit generation can feel really uncomfortable. Although many entrepreneurs consider profit the 'holy grail' of building a business, the process can definitely be personally nerve-wracking. At times, you will need to give yourself pep talks about the importance of value, growth and profit as you intentionally shift your perspective from a doctor to business ownership mindset. The benefits often will not really sink in until you start seeing the changes in the numbers.

A note on volume versus value

Both the costs of being in business and the operating expenses of health care providers are on the rise. Combine that with patients' increased demands for a more personalised and affordable service, and running a profitable medical practice is becoming increasingly difficult. Part of the challenge of running a legally compliant medical practice involves ensuring the practice is viable, and then considering new strategies and patient-care models to increase efficiency and relieve the pressure on the bottom line.

A new opportunity for medical doctors focuses on value-based delivery, which maximises the value of care while also endeavouring to achieve the best possible experience for the patient.

Many doctors respond to the value-based delivery model with confusion. (I can hear your mind ticking over already.) 'Isn't this what we are already doing?' they often ask. You could very well already be working within this model. On the other hand, you might need to consider a shift in focus from the *volume* of patients moving in and out of your clinic to the broader *experience* and *outcomes* achieved. For example, a practice focused on value-based delivery might move away from offering a full range of services because the model is not cost-effective and does not deliver the quality of care expected by patients. The practice might reduce the number of services it provides while working closely with a network of trusted partners to deliver high-value care in specific areas. In the business world, this process is called niching, and by specialising in a practice area, you probably already understand this.

This is not a book about value-based health care, so if you are interested in learning more, Doctor Google can help you find an expert.

NEXT STEPS

I repeatedly meet with clients whose goals don't match their mindset. No amount of tactical learning will 'fix' your business problems if your mindset is creating an insurmountable gap between where you're at and where you want to be.

In this book, I don't ask you to change your mindset. Instead, I ask that you consider what you really want and whether the decisions you've been making are actually designed to reach your goals, and whether your goals are aligned with your mindset.

2 CONTINUING AS THE HIGH ACHIEVER

Success is never final.

Dr George Starr White

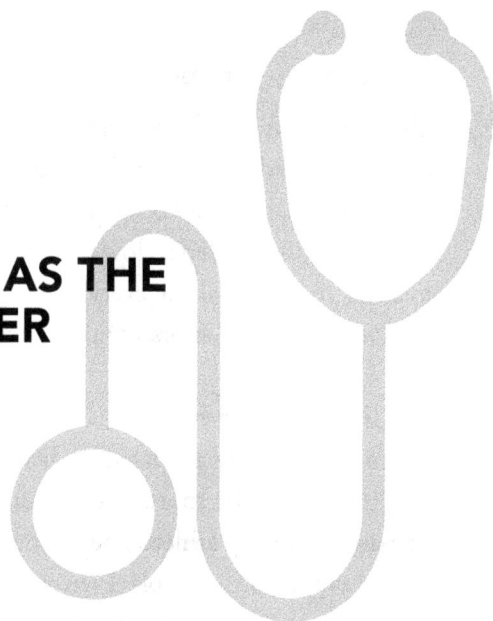

As a doctor, you are inevitably a very high achiever and one of the cleverest people in the room. The traditional metrics of success, wealth and power are likely at your fingertips and, within your circle, you no doubt have a high profile. A certain level of fame follows you as a doctor. As you know, you have been working hard for these indicia of status your whole life. Discipline and rigour guide your daily activities to ensure that patients get the right care – after all, the reason you work so hard is to take care of people.

If you are reading this book, you already have everything you need within you to be successful at business and a high-performing medical practitioner. As you know from the many years you dedicated to study and training, you don't wake up one morning as a doctor. The same goes for each of the subjects in this book. You do not wake up one day an expert at business such as Mark Zuckerberg, the founder of Facebook. Zuckerberg has committed his life to being a business superhero. While I'm not saying you'll need the same commitment, becoming successful in business will take some time.

PREPARE YOUR MINDSET

The importance of preparing your mindset each day cannot be underestimated, and countless studies explain the value of doing so. It's no secret that blockers such as pessimism, distraction, self-doubt, stress, lack of confidence, low self-esteem and fear sabotage and confront medical professionals at every turn in their career. The incredible will to achieve keeps doctors coming back to study more and seek further opportunity.

To perform at your best in your practice, you need to ensure you are psychologically prepared each day. The strategies outlined in this chapter are used by sports and performance experts to aid in the mental preparation of top athletes, performers and business people.

As you read this book, I encourage you to adopt some or all of the following strategies in your day. If you are reading this book, you are interested in creating structures in your practice that mean you can effectively delegate, focus more on your patients and enable you to be both a high-performance medical practitioner and business owner.

The following sections outline the strategies I recommend.

Preparation

There is no substitute for thorough preparation, and many people experience stress if they have not adequately prepared for their day. Preparation can be mundane, like going to sleep early the day before surgery or making sure you have packed lunch and snacks so you have even blood sugar throughout the day. Or it can be more 'big picture' like ensuring you've fully thought through your goals and business plan for your practice.

Helpful, positive thinking

Top performers in any field understand that negative and self-critical thinking creates bad feelings and stress. Pessimism or lack of confidence will transfer across to your team and your patients. Instead, focus on positives and be kind to yourself. Use your thinking to create an attitude of determination, confidence and success. An optimistic approach has been proven to reduce stress and increase feelings of well-being and positivity, and these will likewise be picked up by your patients and team.

Visualisation

Visualisation, also called mental rehearsal, is a powerful psychological strategy used by top performers. Visualise your perfect day while you are still in bed in the morning or before you start the day. Quietly create mental images (see them like a movie running through your mind) of your day going smoothly, and of you performing well and feeling good afterwards. These techniques can help your day become the reality you envisioned. Put in as much detail in as you like. I like to imagine fresh flowers on my kitchen bench as I step through the day in my mind. The visualisation should not be rushed and should contain details such as the clothes you will be wearing and things you will be saying. It should always be positive – you don't want to rehearse anything negative.

It is well worth researching visualisation and using this technique daily, as well as in situations such as interviews, presentations or other performances. If done properly, the brain reacts as though you have really had these positive interview experiences. In addition, research also shows that mental rehearsal decreases stress and increases confidence. I used it to mentally prepare for my wedding (because I have a history of becoming emotionally overwhelmed at times), and I was astounded at the effect it had. This visualisation technique ensured I could be fully present for the whole day.

Relaxation

Relaxation may be easier said than done, but you can reduce stress by keeping your mind and body relaxed – which should not be news to you as a high-performance medical practitioner. So find out what works for you – exercise, meditate, spend time outdoors, get enough quality sleep, eat properly and avoid drugs and alcohol. Something I try to do each day is to practise deep breathing. I find when I am experiencing high stress, I stop breathing deeply and take small, shallow breaths. I notice this reaction sometimes when I am writing, and I always notice it when I am emailing.

Here is how I do the deep breathing: hold each breath for a few seconds and then exhale very, very slowly. Deep breathing reduces the heart rate and lowers blood pressure, so you will immediately feel more relaxed. Do this at any time of stress or when you want to calm yourself. You can even use the deep breathing technique between each patient. It's easy to do, but also hard to remember at times of high stress.

Perseverance

Not every day will go as you want it to, and feeling disappointment about this is understandable, but the mark of every peak performer is being able to move on from disappointments quickly and continue to use positive thinking to keep your confidence up. Note the things you did well, as well as the things you could have done better. Identify changes you can make to improve your performance and move positively into the next challenge.

No matter how you think your day might go or how your day has gone, continue to focus on incorporating all of the techniques from this chapter to build a positive, high-achieving mindset.

PART II

A FLU SHOT FOR YOUR BUSINESS

He who enjoys good health is rich, though he knows it not.

Proverb

It's not just humans who should get a periodic flu shot – you can give your business one too. And just as a flu shot is a preventive act that can help avoid the risk of getting ill, you can put many policies and procedures in place to avoid the risk of your business being destroyed by malpractice, incorrect contracts, insurance policies, or privacy and data breaches.

In the case of your medical business, the 'flu shot' comes in the forms of correct risk assessment and planning, carefully planned contracts and insurance, operations manuals and privacy policies. All these areas, including the risks you may face and your obligations, are covered in the chapters in this part – starting with risk assessment.

3 HOW MEDICAL PROFESSIONALS THINK ABOUT RISK

Every risk is worth taking as long as it is for a good cause, and contributes to a good life.

Richard Branson

As a doctor, you manage a variety of risks every day. You try to manage risk on behalf of your patients – for example, you may sensitively speak to a patient about their weight by asking if it's okay to talk about weight management, even if you know weight *is* an issue the patient came to discuss.

You also manage your own practice risk as per the requirements of your insurance company – by running tests on your patients to confirm or disprove a suspicious set of symptoms, for example. The risk you manage as a medical professional is sharp – it comes into focus every day because it's often a matter of life and death for your patients.

Running a business creates different types of risk and reward. While you have a lot of experience identifying patient and doctor risks, business risks may be more difficult to detect. These risks can be both internal and external to a practice, and they can also directly or indirectly affect the practice's ability to operate. Business perils can be hazard-based (for example, chemical spills), uncertainty-based (natural disasters) or associated with opportunities (the risks involved with taking up an opportunity versus different risks in ignoring it).

The Federal Government's Australian Standard for risk management (AS/NZS ISO 31000:2009) defines risk as 'the chance of something happening that will have an impact on objectives'. I feel like we suddenly got very academic there, sorry. I always aim to speak in plain English, and understand the need for it. (We have a doctor client who had a great opportunity to obtain shares in a start-up. When he received the Option Agreement, he said in an email to me that 'the terminology used in the Agreement is largely inscrutable to me'.) As a lawyer, I'm grateful I'm professionally bi-lingual, but I do understand my role as translator. However, sometimes with the law removing all academic language is just not possible.

So what are the risks that could have an impact on your business objectives? As mentioned, they can be internal and external, as well as direct and indirect. The following sections outline the risks you could face in more detail.

POTENTIAL RISKS TO YOUR BUSINESS

The types of risks that any business faces will be specific to your practice and personal goals but, overall, managing business risk is like managing patient risk. To effectively manage practice risk, you should think about internal and external scenarios that may directly affect your business – and then prepare for them.

As a high-level overview, some common risk categories are:

- natural disasters, such as floods, storms, bushfires and drought
- pandemics, such as human influenza, swine flu or bird flu
- legal issues, such as insurance problems, resolving disputes, contractual breaches, non-compliance with regulations and liabilities
- global events, such as interruptions to air traffic
- technology problems, such as computer network failures and problems associated with using outdated equipment

- regulatory and government policy changes, such as water restrictions, quarantine restrictions, carbon emission restrictions and tax
- environmental changes, such as climate change, chemical spills and pollution
- work health and safety (WHS) issues, such as accidents caused by materials, equipment or location of your work
- property and equipment risks, such as damage from natural disasters, burst water pipes, robbery and vandalism
- security issues, such as theft, fraud, loss of intellectual property, terrorism, extortion, and online security and fraud
- economic and financial changes, such as global financial events, interest rate increases, cash flow shortages, customers not paying, rapid growth and rising costs
- staffing problems, such as industrial relations issues, human error, conflict management and difficulty filling vacancies
- supplier issues, such as problems within their business or industry resulting in failure or interruptions to the supply chain of products or raw materials
- market changes, such as changes in consumer preference and increased competition
- utilities and services issues, such as failures or interruptions to the delivery of your power, water, transport and telecommunications.

Consider using this list as a starting point to think more broadly about the risks that could impact your practice. Also think about other important areas of risks you may need to consider that are not listed here.

INDIRECT RISKS TO YOUR PRACTICE

Overlooking changes and issues that don't directly affect your practice is a common error, and one which can leave you unprepared for change. For example, while your practice might not be directly affected by a natural disaster, you may still suffer if it affects your suppliers, customers or general location.

As an example of this, one of our medical doctor clients recently had an unexpected superstorm hit their town in rural Western Australia. The storm left more than 16,000 homes without power, as well as the local hospital. While the hospital had a generator, our client didn't – and they had vaccines that required refrigeration. So they went to the town's only open hardware store to purchase a generator. Panic broke out when people from other local businesses began scrambling to obtain the last few available generators. Our client managed to procure one of the last generators and the vaccines were saved. If such a widespread power outage had been part of their risk-management plan, they may have already had a generator and may have avoided this stress.

Along similar lines to this doctor's experience, on 26 September 2016 South Australia experienced an almost statewide blackout. (Kangaroo Island was the only place not to lose supply.) Back-up generators were activated at Flinders Medical Centre after the blackout, but stopped working after an hour. Embryos that were being prepared for transfer at a fertility clinic had to be destroyed, with 12 patients affected by the tragedy. South Australia's health minister at the time, Jack Snelling, said scientists were contacted as soon as the power failed and arrived within 20 minutes. 'But without power, there was nothing they could do to save those embryos,' he said.

Unexpected storms can be a timely reminder that we cannot control everything that affects a practice and, therefore, spending the time identifying, assessing, maybe even calculating the probability of certain risks is worthwhile. You can then prioritise which risks your practice should be more prepared for.

Consider how an indirect risk, such as a natural disaster, could affect your practice. For example:

- If your suppliers are affected, you may run out of the items you need to provide proper care to your patients, whether that be drugs, medical instruments or cotton swabs.

- If your patients are personally affected, their priorities may change, and you may experience a reduced demand.

- If your general location is affected, you and your patients may not be able to access your premises, or your utilities could be affected. For example, you could lose power, which could mean you either will not be able to operate your business or may need to throw out any perishable goods and replace them, which can be costly (especially in the case of vaccines).

MANAGING RISK IN YOUR BUSINESS

The process of identifying risks, assessing risks and developing strategies to manage risks is known as risk management. A risk management plan is an essential part of any practice, because it helps you to understand potential risks to your practice and identify ways to minimise them or recover from their consequences.

My second book, *Kingpin: Legal Lessons from the Underworld*, looks in detail at risk management. In writing the book, I had a theory about who the most innovative and creative business leaders of all time might be – while Thomas Edison, Steve Jobs, Nikola Tesla and Bill Gates usually come to mind, I wondered whether it was possible that the most innovative and creative entrepreneurs operated on the fringe of business culture?

Despite the immoral, destructive and violent culture of the illicit drug trade, my research found that drug 'kingpins' are, first and foremost, entrepreneurs and risk managers. These pioneers of the underworld live in an unpredictable and inherently risky world, and face a wealth of diverse business challenges never encountered by our mainstream business leaders.

The most successful kingpins are visionary leaders who survive by implementing effective business strategies and policies. By suspending our judgement of the drug dealer and focusing on the kingpin, we open our minds to their skills, flaws, triumphs and downfalls, all of which are magnified by the volatile environment that shapes their enterprises. This provides us with innovative approaches to managing risk during times of rapid change.

In attempting to manage risk, these leaders of the underworld had to turn to innovation, specialisation, and networking for the success of their business. And, of course, most of the time, their strategies paid off: the reduction of risk contributed to significant profit. While the illicit nature of their enterprises can't be admired, they were undoubtedly successful – and the resulting insights from their successes can be applied by leaders to their own legal businesses. I share some of these insights in the following sections.

Looking at the risks that are relevant to your medical business, risk is measured in terms of likelihood (that is, the probability or frequency) of occurrence and consequences (the outcome or impact of an event) in light of the existing management strategies and controls in place to manage the risk.

A risk procedure for your business will include you considering the consequences of risks materialising that might be negative (hazard risks), positive (opportunity risks) or may result in greater uncertainty. Applying appropriate definitions for the different levels of likelihood and consequences associated with these different risks can be outlined in a likelihood ratings table. This is the first part of your overall risk procedure, and is covered in the following section.

Likelihood ratings

Some events happen once in a lifetime. Others can happen almost every day. Analysing risk requires an assessment of the likely frequency of occurrence. The following table provides broad descriptions used to support likelihood ratings that you can use to create a rating system.

Likelihood rating	Description	Likelihood of occurrence
H	Almost certain	The event is expected to occur in most circumstances
S	Likely	The event will probably occur in most circumstances
M	Possible	The event might occur but, on balance, more likely to occur at some stage
L	Unlikely	The event is not generally expected but could occur at some stage
L	Rare	The event may occur only in exceptional circumstances

Consequence assessment

The next aspect of your risk management system is a consequence assessment. The following table shows an example of one from another organisation. Depending on your tolerance for risk, yours could be similar or vastly different.

Rating	Description	Financial implications	Safety implications	Operational implications – people, systems and processes	Organisational, stakeholder, political reputation implications
1	Catastrophic	Financial loss or potential opportunity loss of greater than $100,000	Life threatening; significant potential for serious personal injury; breach of WHS policy	Catastrophic disruption to business and inability to trade for an extended period of time (5 days or more)	Major embarrassment; media exposure with prominent and sustained coverage
2	Major	Financial loss or potential opportunity loss from $50,000 to $100,000	Potential for serious personal injury; likelihood of breach of WHS policy	Potential disruption to business and inability to trade for a period from 3 to 5 days	Embarrassment
3	Moderate	Financial loss or potential opportunity loss from $10,000 to $49,999	Potential for personal injury; possible breach of WHS policy	Potential disruption to business and inability to trade for a period from 1 to 3 days	Significant stakeholder involvement
4	Minor	Financial loss or potential opportunity loss up to $10,000	Minor potential for injury; required to demonstrate compliance with WHS policy	Potential disruption to business and inability to trade for a period of 1 day	Stakeholder enquiries requiring specific actions
5	Insignificant	No significant financial loss or potential opportunity loss	Negligible safety impact; compliance with WHS policy	No disruption to business continuity	Stakeholder enquiries handled internally

Risk matrix

The next step in your risk management plan is to create a risk matrix, which plots the risk depending on the likelihood and consequence of its occurrence you have identified. An example risk matrix is shown in the following table.

	Consequence				
Likelihood	1 Catastrophic	2 Major	3 Moderate	4 Minor	5 Insignificant
H (almost certain)	H	H	H	S	M
S (likely)	H	H	S	S	M
M (possible)	H	H	S	M	L
L (unlikely)	H	S	M	L	L
L (rare)	S	S	M	L	N

The legend for the risk matrix is shown in the next table.

	Risk level	Action required
H	High risk	Detailed research and management planning at senior level
S	Significant risk	Senior management attention required; immediate action to address issue
M	Moderate risk	Management responsibility must be specified; appropriate action required to address issue
L	Low risk	Manage by routine procedures
N	Negligible risk	No further procedures or action required to address issue

Risk assessment procedure

Once the items outlined in the preceding sections have been considered, a risk assessment procedure can be developed. These are the necessary steps to be completed when assessing and classifying risk:

- recognition or identification of risk
- communication and consultation
- analysis and evaluation of risks
- recording existing and identified risks on the Risk Register to ensure actions are recorded and completed actions documented.

Responding to identified risks

Your options when responding to significant risk are:

- tolerate
- treat
- transfer
- terminate
- consider resourcing controls, including:
  - undertaking internal audits to review processes and functions in relation to identified risks
  - reaction planning
  - reporting and monitoring risk performance.

Framework for managing risk

The following figure outlines a framework for managing risk, based on the international risk guidelines ISO 31000: 2009.

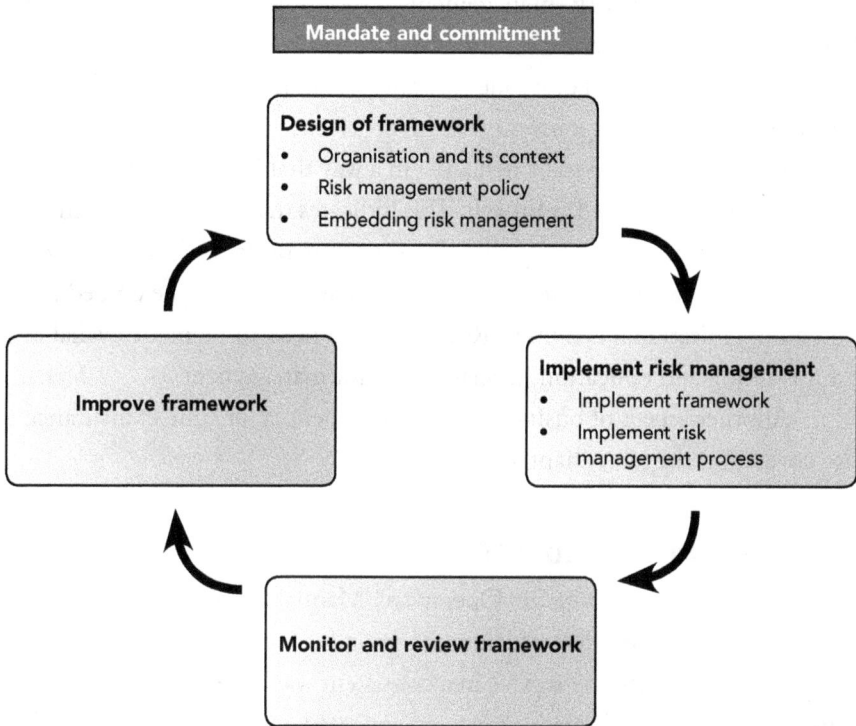

This process needs to be formally conducted across the entire organisation on an ongoing basis in conjunction with business planning and staff meeting discussions.

This sample framework illustrates a 'top-down' and a 'bottom-up' approach to risk management, meaning everyone has a responsibility to continually apply this process when making business decisions and when conducting day-to-day activities.

Training must be provided to staff members at least annually and as necessary.

Result

Risk management is most effective when it is integrated into the culture of an organisation and includes commitment from the leadership team. This culture translates risk strategy into tactical and operational objectives, assigns risk management responsibilities throughout the organisation and supports accountability.

It is important that everyone is aware of their individual and collective risk management responsibilities. In order for risks to be effectively managed, people need to be behaving in a way that is consistent with the organisation's approved approach. This indicates that risk management is not merely about having a well-defined process but also about effecting the behavioural change necessary for risk management to be embedded in all organisational activities. Resources also need to be made available for training and education in relation to risk management.

Another aspect of business risk-management is, of course, insurance – covered in the next chapter.

POLICIES AND PROCEDURES

In addition to preparing an Operations Manual, if you want to grow your practice, and want to enhance your business's ability to deliver high-quality health care service in a consistent way, without dramatically increasing your employees' reliance on you, read on and acquaint yourself with the importance and benefits of written, well-defined Policies and Procedures.

To put it simply, policies and procedures that are well written will allow your team to understand their roles and responsibilities within predefined limits. Policies protect you as the leader because they allow you to guide operations without staff constantly coming to you. So ask yourself…What condition are my practice's written policies and procedures in? In order to understand why policies and procedures are so important we need to know what they are, and the differences between them.

What is a policy?

A 'Policy' is a predetermined course of action, which is established to provide a guide toward accepted business strategies and objectives. In other words, it is a direct link between an organisation's 'Vision' and its day-to-day operations. Policies identify the key activities and provide a general strategy to decision-makers on how to handle issues as they arise. This is accomplished by providing the reader with limits and a choice of alternatives that can be used to 'guide' their decision-making process as they attempt to overcome problems. I like to think of 'policies' as a globe where national boundaries, oceans, mountain ranges and other major features are easily identified.

What is a procedure?

The ultimate goal of every 'Procedure' is to provide the reader with a clear and easily understood plan of action required to carry out or implement a policy. A well-written procedure will also help eliminate common misunderstandings by identifying job responsibilities and establishing boundaries for the jobholders. Good procedures actually allow managers to control events in advance and prevent the organisation (and employees) from making costly mistakes. You can think of a procedure as a road map where the trip details are highlighted in order to prevent a person from getting lost or 'wandering' off an acceptable path identified by the company's management team.

Differentiating between policies and procedures

Policies

- Are general in nature
- Identify rules
- Explain why they exist
- Tell when the rule applies
- Describe who it covers
- Show how the rule is enforced

- Describe the consequences
- Are normally described using simple sentences and paragraphs

Procedures

- Identify specific actions
- Explain when to take actions
- Describe alternatives
- Show emergency procedures
- Include warning and cautions
- Give examples
- Show how to complete forms
- Are normally written using an outline format

Policies and procedures are required when there is a need for consistency in your day-to-day operational activities. Policies and procedures also provide clarity to the reader when dealing with accountability issues or activities that are of critical importance to the company, such as health and safety, legal liabilities, regulatory requirements or issues that have serious consequences.

Are your policies and procedures meeting your needs?

A few 'critical' signs that your policies and procedures need to be reviewed and updated include:

- an increase in the number of accidents, higher failure rates or costly overruns
- more staff questions on 'normal operations' or a feeling of general confusion within a department or division
- employees may also be demonstrating inconsistency in their job performance and there may be an increase in the workforce's stress levels
- customer complaints are increasing.

Benefits of policies and procedures

Now that we have a better understanding of policies and procedures, let's take a look at the major benefits they provide.

- Employees understand the constraints of their job without using a 'trial and error' approach, as key points are visible in well-written policies and procedures.

- Policies and procedures enable the workforce to clearly understand individual and team responsibilities, thus saving time and resources. Everyone is working off the same page; employees can get the 'official' word on how they should go about their tasks quickly and easily.

- Clearly written policies and procedures allow managers to exercise control by exception rather than 'micro-manage' their staff.

- They send a 'We care' message. 'The company wants us to be successful at our jobs.'

- Clearly written policies and procedures provide legal protection. Juries apply the 'common person' standard. If a policy or procedure is written clearly so that outsiders would understand, the company has better legal footing if challenged in court.

Let's return to the first question we asked. Are you interested in growing your business without dramatically increasing your burden of employee management responsibilities? If your answer is yes, we recommend reviewing and implementing policies and procedures that are effective, and work on your company's behalf.

4 CONTRACTS AND INSURANCE

A healthy outside starts from the inside.

Robert Urich

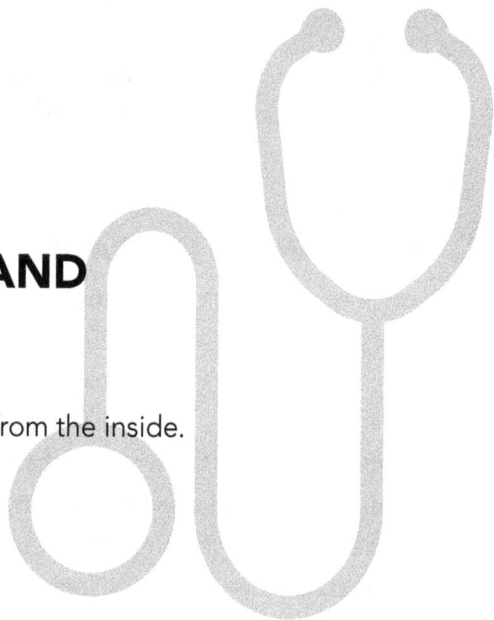

I recently heard someone say that a business is a series of contracts and agreements, and I think this is such an accurate description. Agreements exist between the practice and its staff, its landlord, its suppliers, its bank – the list goes on. Of course, this is likely not news to you, and no doubt it is also not news to you that, while some agreements and contracts are documented in writing, others are not.

Contracts are the basis for everyday transactions and whether an agreement is put in writing is usually dependent on the type of agreement being entered into. In particular, those agreements that are discrete, one-off exchanges of a minor nature and do not require ongoing obligations between the parties are often only made by word of mouth and are not in writing.

Where the contract is more significant in terms of financial exposure, commitment or risk, putting its terms in writing is prudent, because this will enable both parties to understand their rights and obligations, and provide evidence of the terms of the agreement if a dispute arises.

Insurance is another type of business agreement, and one that should be a key part of your business risk management, so I also discuss the kinds of areas you should be covered for at the end of this chapter.

UNDERSTANDING CONTRACTS

Let's start at the very beginning with contracts (after all, it's a very good place to start). So, what is a contract? A contract is a set of promises made between two or more parties that gives rise to legal obligations to do particular things. With the intent to create a legal relationship, parties are able to enforce the terms of the contract and claim damages where promises made under these terms have not been fulfilled.

A contract does not need to be in writing for it to be legally binding or enforceable by law – as long as the parties to the contract have expressed the intention to create a legal relationship and understand their obligations in doing so. However, without a written agreement, proving what was initially agreed upon can be difficult if a dispute arises at a later date. Often some uncertainty will emerge as to the exact terms that were agreed upon, particularly for more complicated agreements, and because no objective evidence exists, it will often be one party's word against the other. This all makes the actual terms that were agreed very difficult to establish. Putting the agreed terms down in writing, therefore, is advisable because it provides reliable evidence to establish that a contract exists and identifies the exact terms that were agreed.

Knowing the precise terms of a contract is also important because parties can then understand their obligations in greater detail and what it is they are required to do. This also reduces the likelihood of a dispute arising because the parties are able to see what has been agreed to in writing, and not form vastly different interpretations of their obligations. While an oral agreement may also be clear in its terms, these terms are at risk of being distorted from what was originally agreed upon, particularly where the contract has been varied many times since it was formed or it was made a long time ago.

For long-term relationships between parties, written contracts are also necessary in preserving the social relationship. This is because the parties are expected to behave in a way that aligns with their obligations under the contract. Contracts spanning over a long period are also likely to be varied over time and so it is important that the parties are certain of their roles within these changes, and can effectively track all the changes made in the interests of avoiding disputes and protecting the contractual and broader social relationship between the parties.

Written agreements are also useful in protecting the more vulnerable party within more important transactions with larger parties. This is because the written agreement draws the attention of the vulnerable party to all the terms that may not be considered or may be overlooked in an oral contract. These include any harsh or unfair terms and the potential consequences of exiting the agreement.

Lastly, some contracts are only acceptable in writing due to their importance – for example, contracts such as assignments and mortgages of life insurance policies and transactions relating to land are otherwise void if they are not in writing.

Despite oral and written contracts both having the ability to create a legally binding relationship, written contracts provide a number of benefits that oral contracts do not. In comparing the effectiveness of oral and written contracts, an agreement in writing is clearly essential for clarifying expectations between the parties and providing greater legal protection and assurance that the promises made are upheld. So get your agreements in writing.

15 THINGS TO LOOK AT WHEN REVIEWING A CONTRACT

This chapter is intended to help you review contracts so you will know what you are signing before you sign it. Periodically reviewing existing contracts such as insurance policies, leases and banking documents to determine whether they still meet your needs is also good practice. And don't be afraid to get an expert to assist with reviewing or drafting contracts on your behalf.

In its most basic form, a contract is merely an agreement between two or more people to do or not do a particular thing. That sounds simple enough, but when those obligations are buried in the fine print in the middle of a lengthy document, understanding exactly what the parties are agreeing to do or not do may not be so easy.

So, what should you look for when reviewing a contract? The following sections outline a few suggestions.

Negotiate the terms

When presented with a contract, remember that this is a starting point. You can negotiate the terms of nearly every agreement. You want to make the deal happen, but so does the other person. Ask for what you want. The worst that can happen is they say no. Some parties will not, on principle, negotiate some terms of some agreements – for example, banks can be very hard to negotiate with on specific contract terms. Understanding the tolerance of the other party for negotiating is a whole other skill.

Identify the parties

Correctly identify the parties. Use the complete name of the business to avoid confusion and identify the director or company secretary as such. Determine the marital status of individuals if spouses will be required to join in execution of the document, and also think about who will sign and witness the agreement. In some cases it is not appropriate for people who are related to each other to witnessing each other's signatures – an example of this would be a personal guarantee where, if both husband and wife were entering into personal guarantees, it may not be appropriate for them to witness each other's signatures.

Complete all blanks

Complete all blanks on any pre-printed form because items left blank can be filled in later by someone else. Be sure all changes or deletions are initialled.

Double check the business terms

Double check the business terms of the contract (price, amount, duration, square footage and so on) to determine whether it accurately reflects the agreement of the parties.

Automatic renewals

Look for automatic renewals. Do you have to give notice if you do not want to renew? Are there penalties if notice is not timely given? Is renewal on the same terms as the original agreement? Are there price increases? Consider adding options to renew on favourable terms. Also make sure you diarise these clauses, so as not to get trapped into an agreement for an additional term if the agreement is no longer serving you.

Allocating risk

Determine how risk is to be allocated. Risk is typically borne by the party in the best position to prevent loss. However, there may be reasons for a different allocation. Check insurance requirements. Will you be able to obtain the required insurance within your budget?

Indemnification provisions

Check to see if any indemnification provisions exist. When you indemnify someone, you are agreeing to protect them from liability or loss that may arise out of the transaction. If you must indemnify the other party, limit the indemnification as much as possible. Negotiate the same indemnification for yourself. For instance, if you, as buyer, agree to indemnify the seller of a business for losses they may incur as a result of actions after the sale, they should indemnify you for losses you may incur as a result of actions before the sale.

Incorporated documents

When another document is incorporated by reference always read the incorporated document. Don't assume you know what it contains.

Events of default

Determine what acts constitute events of default and whether you are able to enter into and perform under the contract without causing a default. Also consider what should be included as events of default by the other party.

Remedies provisions

Review remedies provisions. Determine the worst that can happen to you if you default. Explore ways to limit your liability. Also determine what types of remedies you need in the event of default by the other party.

Causes for termination

Review causes for termination. Consider including ways to terminate the contract if it is not working to your benefit.

Dates and deadlines

Check dates and deadlines. Always keep a calendar of dates and deadlines for important events and anything required to be done by you or the other party.

Warranties and representations

Review and understand warranties and representations given by you and the other party. Don't give any representation if you do not actually know that the representation is true or if the other party is in a better position to know the facts being represented. If you must give warranties, try to limit them as much as possible. For example, a warranty in a deed might say that you warrant title to the property. You can limit the warranty by saying that you warrant title to the property only during the period of time in which you owned the property. Remember that the other party is trying to do the same, so watch for disclaimers or limitations.

Rights and responsibilities

Know all of your rights and responsibilities under the contract. Carefully read the entire contract because rights and responsibilities are typically scattered throughout the agreement.

Resolution of disputes

Determine how you want to deal with resolution of disputes. An arbitration or mediation requirement could ultimately save you lots of time and money. However, at times you may need to go to court to resolve the dispute. When appropriate, try to give yourself some flexibility.

PROCESS FOR NEGOTIATING CONTRACTS

The preceding sections provide a limited list of general provisions to consider when entering into a contract. The type of transaction that is the basis of the contract, as well as the relative bargaining positions of the parties will dictate the actual terms of the agreement. If you take the time to thoroughly review and negotiate the terms of your contracts before you sign, you should find, in the long run, that it is time well spent.

Even with the provisions already provided, I still often observe my medical professional clients muddling through contract negotiations. To further assist you in the future, I have provided a list of the five most common errors made by doctors at the bargaining table.

Willingness to accept unfairness

Fighting for justice and equality are part of a lawyer's job description – and I'll admit I'm pretty comfortable engaging in battle. I have noticed, however, that my medical professional clients are not always as passionate about a fight. If you do not like conflict, you may be unable to sufficiently protect your interests while negotiating a contract, which makes you more likely to accept terms that are unfair, or in some cases, against the law.

Failure to appreciate the hidden costs

Wordy clauses, such as contingent liability provisions, are often positioned deep in a contract and, therefore, may go unnoticed and/ or survive contract negotiations without objection or comment. A contingent liability clause can, however, create significant and unexpected obligations for doctors in the future. Additional clauses that doctors should, but often do not, dispute are restraint and liquidated damages clause.

What is a *liquidated damages* clause? I'm so glad you asked. It's a provision in a contract that requires a breaching party to pay huge amounts of money when a certain event occurs that has been identified in advance as an occurrence that warrants an award of liquidated damages.

A *restraint of trade* clause is commonly found in an employment or contractor agreement, or a shareholder's or partnership agreement, and they are most commonly used by parties to try to protect their business interests (for example, customer or patient relationships). The restraints can vary, but as a general rule they include at least one of the following:

- confidential information and trade secrets may not be used
- prohibition to work for a competitor for a period after the employee/shareholder leaves the business
- prohibition to solicit clients, staff and customers from the business.

Failure to do the necessary background research

Most doctors are highly empathetic and trusting. In addition, because a doctor's time is extremely valuable, doctors often do not want to spend much time discussing contract terms or issues. When a doctor is presented with a contract to review and sign, he or she will often accept the oral representations of the other party to the contract without verifying those representations were accurately translated in writing. Doctors may not read all the details of the contract and may assume the other party to the contract will perform the obligations of the contract as promised.

Doctors should instead adopt a business mindset and take the time to review and analyse the written terms of the business opportunity and research the other parties to the contract. Careful consideration of the contract terms and parties can raise previously unknown or undisclosed issues, provide a more accurate estimate of a party's ability to perform the contract, and allow you to make a more informed decision on whether to agree or object to the inclusion of the terms.

Failure to read or understand the fine print

Many of my doctor clients see contract provisions as 'a lot of words'. While this may be true, the words in legal contracts are designed to convey very specific meanings in a court room setting, and the meaning of a word is generally designed to protect the person or company that drafted or presented you with the contract. When the parties to a contract do not negotiate its terms, it is less likely to be fair and even-handed.

Failure to seek expert assistance or advice

Sometimes medical professionals fear that involving a lawyer in contract negotiations will alienate the other party or give the impression the doctor is either afraid or lacks business savvy. On the contrary, I have found that doctors who consult legal counsel on contract matters can often expedite negotiations by initiating a clean, fair and professional relationship with the other party, which also sets a good tone for amicable and healthy future dealings.

Contract provisions can be confusing because they often involve complex issues and unforeseen risks. Negotiating contract terms that serve the clients' interests is a skill that requires talent, knowledge and experience. Delegating tasks outside your expertise, such as contract negotiations, allows you to focus your energy on patient care and reduces the stress of micro-managing every aspect of a private practice.

WORKING THROUGH INSURANCE

Business insurance is the most direct way to protect against unexpected risks in your business; however (disclaimer), I do not profess to be an expert in insurance. This section provides a quick overview of the main types of insurance you're likely to need for your medical business. For more information, and cover tailored to your personal circumstances, talk with your financial planner and insurance broker.

As a professional service provider, I've no doubt you already know how important it is to carry professional indemnity insurance. However, you might also need to consider other types of business insurance, but what kind of coverage do you need? The following are some areas to consider:

- Because you employ people, you will require workers compensation insurance. If you're unsure whether you're already paying for this, you can confirm with your bookkeeper or accountant. Chances are you personally will be covered by this policy as well for any injury that may occur to your employees during the time they are working for you.

- If as part of your practice you sell products, you could also consider product liability insurance. You can contact a business insurance broker to discuss this further. Some brokers specialise in medical professionals, so search online or check with a colleague to find a recommended broker.

- Personal insurances you might like to consider include income protection, life insurance, total and permanent disability (TPD) insurance, critical illness or trauma insurance. These are the jurisdiction of financial planners and banks, or can be arranged via insurance companies directly.

- If you're operating your business as a company (which is the most likely scenario – see chapter 9), you may consider taking out directors' and officers' liability insurance. This is not compulsory but may be worthwhile, depending on your situation. In my first book, *How to Avoid a Fall from Grace: Legal Lessons for Directors*, I discuss the duties and obligations directors have in more detail.

- If you own your own building, you need to consider building insurance. Regardless of whether or not you own the building where you practice, you should have contents insurance in place. Again, check with your financial planner and insurance broker if you have any questions in this area.

One important aspect to note is that your medical indemnity insurance will not cover you for general business risks – such as employee theft and privacy breaches. I delve into these and other risks in the following chapters.

5 OPERATIONS MANUALS AND DISCLAIMERS

Life with its rules, its obligations, and its freedoms, is like a sonnet: you're given the form, but you have to write the sonnet yourself.

Madeleine L'Engle

Do not skip over this chapter. I know, I know, the very thought of developing a useful operations manual and well-worded disclaimers for a medical practice can give you a headache. But the enormity of the task becomes much less with a clear understanding of the objectives of why creating an operations manual should be a priority and some simple tools to help you make it come to life. Taking the plunge to create an operations manual and worthwhile disclaimers is also a fantastic opportunity to advance the goal of making your business legally compliant. First, let's tackle your operations manual.

WRITING YOUR OPERATIONS MANUAL: STRUCTURES, SYSTEMS AND POLICIES

In any business, an operations manual supports and reinforces staff training and serves as a ready reference. This is especially useful when:

- a subject matter expert is not in the office
- a change needs to be implemented and it's important to avoid unintended consequences.

At the risk of stating the obvious, an operations manual should be well organised, neat and accurate. It must be internally consistent because it is going to be the definitive authority on the standards of the practice. If you are planning to build your practice for sale, this document is going to be an investment in growing the value of your practice.

Let's face it, your operations manual is not going to win a Booker Prize, so simple words and short sentences are more important than engaging prose. You should also understand that an operations manual, like a business, is a work in progress. It needs to be constantly updated and corrected because circumstances and the practice environment are constantly changing. One way to think about it is this: an operations manual without annotation is probably not being used very well – so making a point to quarterly or bi-annually review and update the manual is a good idea. Trying to keep it 'perfect' and unchanged, on the other hand, is likely to make your team put it in the 'too hard' basket and abandon it.

Even with simple, short sentences, your operations manual is likely to have a significant word count, simply because of the number of areas you need to cover. One way to make the task less daunting is to take the advice of Maria from *The Sound of Music* and start at the very beginning, which (as she highlights and I've already mentioned) is a very good place to start. So start with the basics and pull together your Table of Contents, trying to think of all the areas you'll likely need to cover. Medical practice operations are complicated, and knowing where to start may be very difficult. A potential draft Table of Contents can give a useful framework and discrete tasks, which can make the overall task more manageable. I have included a sample Table of Contents for your operations manual in appendix A. You can use this as a base and then personalise it for your business.

Cobbling together all the information required in your operations manual will be a lot of work, and this includes gathering the content that already exists. Look around the office. Lists of all sorts of things are likely posted at each workstation, and individual employees will have their own private notes. The best person to ask is probably your most recently hired employee. Why? Well, their notes from their training will be the most congruent with the business's most up-to-date practices.

Even this initial gathering of information can help make the information circulating within your staff more worthwhile and consistent. If the information that you gather is accurate, it is valuable and it will be worthwhile making it available to everyone in the practice. If not, the team need to know and it needs to be stamped out. You may also find this a great opportunity to ask staff to describe what they actually do. In the process of doing their day-to-day work, your team can also record the steps, thereby creating procedures. The objective at this point is to capture as much as is practical without making the task so burdensome it is abandoned. Remember – missed steps can be added later, and also remember that the creation of this document is adding value to your practice.

Content reconciliation at this stage is critical. If you are looking for someone to champion the cause, to be honest anyone on staff can accumulate the material, but make sure that the responsible doctor reviews and reconciles it – both initially, and at regular intervals – please do not wait until the end to undertake the review. In almost every review, the doctor will uncover something they did not know about what is really going on in their practice. Even though it may not seem like a priority, this creates a wonderful opportunity to discuss discrepancies with the team, to gather their input and come to agreements on how things should be done that are acceptable to everyone.

A practical tip – if you are working with the operations manual as an electronic document, the 'Track Changes' feature in Microsoft Word is useful. If you don't already know, this tool records who added or changed information and the date the change was made, while preserving the original information. (Just make sure all staff know to leave Track Changes switched on.)

While it's not a legal requirement, an operations manual is a hugely valuable tool for optimal practice profitability, productivity and risk mitigation. It can also be developed and maintained without a big investment of practice time and energy. What is required to develop a functional operations manual is a clear view of its function, and an acceptance that it will never be perfect or completed.

DISCLAIMERS

Technology has taken over our everyday lives and has revolutionised all areas of business. While some professions have been slower to utilise new technology than others (the legal profession is notoriously slack), it's no secret that technology is here to stay.

Information tech, in particular, has had an enormous impact on business practices. If your practice has a website or you use email, you need to consider the use of disclaimers in your business. The three important disclaimers to think about are covered in the following sections.

Website

If you have a website, you should ensure your website terms and conditions and privacy policy are kept up to date. The website terms and conditions could contain a disclaimer, or you could have disclaimers on different pages of your website depending on what the content is. While we are talking about websites, your website is a very convenient place to locate your Privacy Policy (covered in more detail in the next chapter).

Email

We use email technology so frequently now that the risks associated with using standard unencrypted emails is not always obvious. However, in the health care environment, patient privacy must be prioritised. Doctors are receiving increased requests from patients, other clinicians and third parties for health information to be transmitted electronically. Accommodating those requests, however, creates a risk of breaching a patient's privacy. Doctors need to ensure that the electronic methods they use to transmit a patient's medical records are adequately safe and secure. As all health information is sensitive by nature, all communications of health information, including via electronic means, must adequately protect the patient's privacy.

As a first step in this, a disclaimer should be placed at the bottom of each email. I recommend using the following text.

Email disclaimer

This email, and any attachments, are proprietary and confidential and are intended solely for the use of the individual to whom it is addressed. If you have received this email in error, please let us know immediately by replying to this email and deleting it from your system. You may not use, disseminate, distribute or copy this message nor disclose its contents to anyone.

We value online security and undertake all reasonable steps to ensure our emails and attachments are virus-free. Unfortunately, emails can be corrupted without our knowledge. Recipients should always check emails and attachments for viruses and delete any corrupted material.

Any views or opinions expressed are solely those of the author and do not necessarily reflect or represent those of [insert practice name].

The agents and employees of [insert practice name] are not authorised to enter into any binding agreement or contract on behalf of [insert practice name] without express written consent from a Director.

Please do not print this email unless it is necessary. Every unprinted email saves our trees.

Brochures and marketing materials

Whether you print brochures, write a blog, or publish videos or other marketing materials online, you should include a disclaimer with this content. Without assessing the specific content of these materials, making a recommendation of what to cover in the disclaimer is difficult. However, you should be aware of the need for disclaimers and consider them an opportunity to manage risk in the future. Take a sample of similar published content that includes a disclaimer and use this to draft your own – and, of course, if you have any questions or doubts, check with a lawyer.

6 PRIVACY POLICIES AND DATA PROTECTION

The best time to plant a tree was 20 years ago.
The second best time is now.

Chinese Proverb

Given the sensitive nature of information medical practitioners have access to, it is no surprise that they are subject to some of the most stringent privacy rules of any sector. Privacy is serious business. Cyber security experts estimate that a single medical record is worth US$1000 on the dark net, and hackers are working hard to cash in – even if you have 100 patients on your list, for example, that's an attractive salary for a day's work.

But it's not just hackers and criminals looking to cash in. Legitimate businesses acting as data brokers are very adept at collecting personal and sensitive information and on-selling it in an industry that is worth more than $450 million a year.

This is directly affecting medical businesses. Of the total complaints received by the Office of the Australian Information Commissioner (OAIC) in 2016, 10 per cent related to health service providers, and only 40 per cent of patients surveyed by the OAIC fully trust their medical practitioner with their sensitive health information. The OAIC estimates that more than 10 per cent of practices don't even have a privacy policy in place.

In this environment, it is not surprising that the Australian government is taking data protection very seriously. *The Privacy Act 1988* (Cth) (the 'Act') sets out the laws relating to the collection, storage and use of personal and sensitive information, along with the Australian Privacy Principles (APPs). The Privacy Act is administered by the OAIC, which has the power to investigate and bring charges for breaches of the Act, with fines of up to $1.8 million for a breach by a corporation and $340,000 for a breach by an individual. With stakes as high as these, privacy and data protection is definitely an area you need to be across in your medical business and incorporate into policies. In this chapter, I take you through all the aspects you should be aware of, starting with privacy.

UNDERSTANDING TERMS AND OBLIGATIONS

The Privacy Act and its APPs include some jargon and terms that may seem confusing. So first let's run through some of the terms and principles, and what they all mean.

What is an APP Entity?

An entity that must comply with the Privacy Act and the Australian Privacy Principles is referred to as an APP Entity. An APP entity includes any organisation with an annual turnover of more than $3 million along with specific classes of organisations such as government agencies, operators of residential tenancies databases and health service providers.

Health service providers are defined very broadly in the Act and include any organisation that diagnoses or treats illnesses, records health information for the purpose of assessing, maintaining or improving a person's health, and even dispenses a drug or medicine.

What is personal and sensitive information?

Personal information is defined in the Act as information or an opinion, whether true or not and whether recorded in a material form or note, about an identified individual or an individual who is reasonably identifiable. This may include information provided by your patients such as their name, address, email and telephone number.

Sensitive information includes any information about an individual's racial or ethnic origin, political or religious affiliations, sexual preference or practices, criminal records, health information, genetic information or biometric information.

Sensitive information is subject to much stricter obligations for collection use and disclosure.

What do the Privacy Principles cover?

In the Act, 13 Privacy Principles set out how APP Entities must deal with personal information.

The principles are not prescriptive – each entity must also consider how the principles apply in practice to their business and the information they handle. However, the principles will apply much more stringently to entities that collect and store sensitive information.

The APPs are:

- *APP1: Open and transparent.* Entities must manage personal information in an open and transparent manner. This includes having an up-to-date Privacy Policy displayed on your website and/ or available on request in your practice.

- *APP2: Anonymity.* Individuals must have the opportunity to remain anonymous and/or use a pseudonym when dealing with the APP Entity. The requirement to fulfil this APP has some exceptions – such as where dealing with an individual on an anonymous basis is not practicable.

- *APP3: Collection of solicited personal information.* This principle sets out the circumstances in which entities may collect information. An entity may only collect personal information if it is reasonably necessary for them to undertake their function. The collection of sensitive information must be reasonably necessary, and the entity must also obtain consent before doing so. For medical practitioners, it is generally accepted that a patient seeking medical care consents to the collection of their health information for that purpose.

- *APP4: Dealing with unsolicited personal information.* This principle sets out what an entity should do with any personal information they receive, but did not request. In circumstances where the entity would not be permitted to collect such information, they must take immediate steps to destroy or de-identify it.

- *APP5: Notification of the collection of personal information.* If you collect information about a patient, you must notify them at the time, or as soon as reasonably possible after the collection of the information. In most circumstances, this would be implicit in the nature of the doctor–patient relationship. There may be circumstances, however, where you would be required to first seek the consent of your patient, such as when requesting medical files from a previous practitioner.

- *APP6: Use and disclosure of personal information.* APP entities may only use or disclose personal information for the purpose it was collected. The only purpose in which sensitive health information should be used, for example, is to obtain medical treatment. It would be a gross breach of both the Privacy Act and your professional obligations to use or disclose sensitive patient information for any other purpose.

- *APP7: Direct Marketing.* An APP may use or disclose sensitive information for the purposes of direct marketing in only extremely limited circumstances. Unless your patient has expressly consented, you should not be using sensitive information for marketing purposes.

- *APP8: Cross border disclosure.* If you disclose information to an overseas recipient, you must take reasonable steps to ensure that the recipient of that information will comply with the Australian Privacy Principles, or have grounds to reasonably believe that the recipient is subject to a law or scheme that has a similar effect in protecting the personal information.

- *APP9: Government identifiers.* Government identifiers are the unique numbers assigned to an individual by a government department. They include tax file numbers and Medicare numbers. This principle prevents an entity from adopting any identifier as its own identifier. This means you cannot record or refer to your patients by their Medicare number. If you use identifiers in your practice, you must adopt your own unique identifier. APP9 also states that you must not disclose a government identifier unless permitted by the Act.

- *APP10: Quality of personal information.* You must take reasonable steps to ensure that any information you collect is accurate, up to date and complete.

- *APP11: Security.* You must take reasonable steps to protect personal information from misuse, interference, loss and unauthorised access.

- *APP12: Access to personal information.* The general rule provides that, if an individual requests their personal information, you must provide them with access. This general rule has several exceptions, however, including where providing the information would result in a threat to health or safety, the information is the subject of legal proceedings or other enforcement activities, or where disclosure would be unlawful.

- *APP13: Correction of personal information.* The final principle provides that, if you hold information which you believe to be incorrect or incomplete, or where the individual requests you to do so, you must update the record to ensure that it is complete and accurate.

These Privacy Principles should be reflected in your privacy policy, and built into the daily processes and procedures of your practice.

NOTIFIABLE DATA BREACHES SCHEME

In business, as in life, we all understand that sometimes things can go wrong. Unfortunately, when data protection goes wrong it can have serious flow-on consequences for patients.

In addition to the Privacy Principles already covered in this chapter, practitioners must also be aware and understand their obligations under the Notifiable Data Breaches Scheme.

The Notifiable Data Breaches Scheme requires APP entities to notify both the OAIC and any affected individuals where an eligible data breach is likely to result in serious harm. It also requires APP entities to undertake a full assessment of suspected data breaches.

An eligible data breach occurs where an unauthorised access, disclosure or loss of personal information has occurred, where the loss is likely to result in serious harm.

In some cases, the access, disclosure or loss may be very clear – for example, you leave your laptop (with stored patient files) on the train. Unauthorised access may be your IT system alerting you that you have been hacked and patient files have been downloaded.

In other cases, the breach might not be so very clear – for example, when you check the login data of your patient management files and see that the new intern has been viewing patient files. This may not, from the given facts, be an unauthorised access, particularly if you requested her to review some files. In certain circumstances, however, her access may not be authorised. Perhaps it appears she has been searching the database for files with a specific name and you cannot think of any legitimate reason for her to be searching for those files. Or perhaps your IT guru notices something funky happening. He determines that your systems have been infected with a virus but is not sure whether data has in fact been compromised or accessed.

This is where it can get tricky. However, if you have reasonable grounds to suspect that a data breach may have occurred, you must undertake an assessment and complete it within 30 days – and the clock starts as soon as the potential breach comes to your attention.

Your assessment should include three stages:

1 *Initiate:* If you suspect a data breach, immediately initiate an assessment. Appoint a person responsible for the assessment.

2 *Investigate:* Gather as much information as possible relating to the possible breach.

3 *Evaluate:* Responsible person looks at all the information and decides whether a notifiable data breach has occurred.

If you determine an eligible data breach has not occurred, you should record your assessment and finding, and update any processes or policies necessary to prevent a data issue of that kind occurring in the future.

If you determine that a data breach has occurred, you should proceed to determining whether that breach is likely to result in serious harm for one or more people whose information has been lost – the second element of the Notifiable Data Breaches Scheme.

In deciding whether the breach is likely to result in serious harm, you must consider the following points:

• Harm is not limited to physical harm. It might be physiological, emotional, reputational, or something else.

• The potential harm must be serious.

• The potential must be more likely than not.

The question of whether the loss or unauthorised access of personal information is likely to result in serious harm is objective. This means you must consider the scenario as presented to you and make a reasonable determination based only on the facts. Considerations may include:

• What sort of personal information is involved? Was it sensitive health information or their Netflix download history?

• Who has the information? Was it downloaded by a hacker, or does the intern have it?

• Is the data encrypted or password protected by two-factor authentication?

- How long has this access been possible? Is it a very recent thing or have you just realised that every intern since 1999 has had unauthorised access?

If in doubt, workshop potential harm

If you're still struggling to work out whether the potential harm is serious enough for you to report, workshop a few different situations. Consider the following scenarios and what you may need to ask yourself:

- *Scenario:* While doing some (authorised) work, your intern stumbled across a file with a rare medical condition and, despite not having authority, she was curious and viewed the file.
- *Ask yourself:* Is this likely to result in serious harm?
- *Scenario:* Your external back-up drive with all your patient files was in your briefcase, which you left on the train.
- *Ask yourself:* Is this likely to result in serious harm? What if the data is encrypted?
- *Scenario:* Your night security cameras catch your cleaning personnel using your computer.
- *Ask yourself:* What if the access records log reveals he has downloaded the health records of several local prominent personalities? What if the server reveals he tried to access the database and couldn't get past the password?
- *Scenario:* You accidentally email a patient's health declaration containing their name, address and birthdate to another unrelated medical practitioner.
- *Ask yourself:* Would your answer change if you sent the file to another patient? What if the declaration contained specific information relating to a sensitive medical condition? What if you are the only GP in a very small town?

Determining the remedial action required

Once you have determined that unauthorised access, disclosure or loss has occurred and that the loss is likely to result in serious harm, you need to consider whether you can implement any immediate remedial action that will prevent the risk of harm.

This is an important step, because if your remedial action prevents risk of harm, this issue ceases to be a notifiable data breach.

Let's consider one of the workshop scenarios from the preceding section: You accidentally email a patient's health declaration containing their name, address and birthdate to another unrelated medical practitioner. Here, you have several possible outcomes.

The medical professional acknowledges receipt of the email and that they viewed the files, but advises that they immediately deleted the email upon realising that it did not relate to one of their patients. You trust the medical practitioner's professional ethics and determine that it is extremely unlikely that your patient will suffer any harm from the mistake. No breach has occurred.

Alternatively, you practice in a small town and the email contains a declaration of a very sensitive medical condition relating to another patient. You email the medical professional immediately and receive the response that they have read the file and know the patient involved – and they are concerned because your patient is working with children.

In this scenario, your remedial action is not sufficient to reduce the likely risk of harm to your patient and the breach is notifiable.

The Notifiable Data Breaches Scheme is still very new and some aspects of it will remain vague until we start seeing matters brought by the OAIC. Some things, however, are certain: remedial action will only prevent a notifiable data breach if the action was taken before any relevant person suffered harm.

Notification

Once you determine that a notifiable data breach has occurred and your remedial action hasn't been enough to prevent the likely risk of harm, you must follow through on the notification requirements as set out in the Act, as soon as possible. You must notify all relevant persons of the breach, using your usual method of communication, whether that is phone, email or post.

If you are unable to contact the relevant persons, you must prominently display the details of the breach on your website. Depending on the circumstances, you may need to also publish details in social media or print media. If you do not have contact details and only deal with people in person, you must place a prominent notice in your shop or practice.

Your notice should contain an apology and any practical steps that patients might be able to take to mitigate their risk of harm. This usually involves things like changing passwords, perhaps on their My Health Record or My Gov account, and cancelling credit cards or other payment information.

Remember – transparency and empathy are the key attributes of managing a data breach.

Completing an OAIC statement

Along with notifying all relevant persons of the breach, you must also complete an OAIC statement. This is an online form available on the OAIC website that asks you to include the following:

- identity and contact details of your organisations
- a description of the eligible breach
- the kinds of information involved
- what practical steps you recommend individuals may take to protect themselves from or mitigate the harm.

Exceptions to the notification rules

Some very limited exceptions apply to the requirement to notify after a breach has occurred. These include where a breach applies to multiple entities, where notification would be likely to prejudice law enforcement or where an exception has been granted by the Commissioner on public interest grounds.

One final exception is possible for medical practitioners – where a reportable breach has occurred under the My Health Records Act.

If you are a participant in the My Health Records systems, and a reportable data breach has occurred that comes under the My Health Records Act that needs to be reported to either the Systems Operator or the OAIC, you do *not* need to also report the breach under the Notifiable Data Breaches Scheme.

This exception is to avoid duplication of notice requirements.

If, however, a breach involves the practice clinical database or other records not covered by the My Health Records Act, and serious harm is likely, the breach will need to be reported under the Notifiable Data Breaches Scheme.

WHAT STEPS SHOULD I NOW TAKE?

A 'one size fits all' solution can't be applied to privacy compliance, but every practice can take two universal steps:

1 regularly review your processes and keep your privacy policy up to date

2 train your staff in privacy compliance, including how to recognise and respond to suspected data breaches.

PART III

X-RAY FOR YOUR BUSINESS: SEARCHING FOR HIDDEN FRACTURES

Success is the progressive realisation of enjoying good health.

Deepak Chopra

Although many professional service providers claim to be 'in the business of helping people', only medical professionals truly take care of people in matters of life or death. Saving lives requires intense training, mental focus and commitment. So it's perhaps no surprise that many doctors have a difficult time pivoting from the intensity of patient care to the ambiguity of business care.

If you are in the mode to 'Ready, Set, Grow' your business, you've reached the right part of the book. The chapters in this part aim to bring your business into sharper focus, holding up operations to the x-ray machine and searching for any fractures as we consider financial metrics, the errors that can kill a medical business, your business structure and shareholder agreement, and your intellectual property.

With the right business strategy, operational efficiencies and structure in place, you can be confident your practice will stay on track – and even grow – while you dedicate yourself to the consuming work of taking care of patients.

7 WHAT DOES A HEALTHY MEDICAL BUSINESS LOOK LIKE?

To know even one life has breathed easier because you have lived. This is to have succeeded.

Ralph Waldo Emerson (American Essayist)

One of the biggest challenges of owning a private practice is juggling patient care with the needs of a business in a demanding marketplace. You know how to heal patients, but how do you tend to the needs of your medical practice? Patient and business health may have more in common than you think. To help clarify the connection, let's borrow a trick from the medical trade – preventative care.

No doubt you instruct patients to undertake a variety of activities to help develop strong bodies and minds – for example, eating right, exercising and getting eight hours of sleep. You know that if your patients make healthy lifestyle changes, they increase the likelihood of avoiding or overcoming a medical problem arising in the future. Before you can recommend preventative care, however, you need to assess the overall condition of the patient's health.

The same theory applies to your medical business. How can you tell if your practice is healthy? From time to time, you should assess your business's wellbeing, and one way to do that is to look at its financial metrics. So, what are these metrics? 'Metrics' refers to measurement, and can include software performance metrics and customer satisfaction metrics, along with what I am going to talk about in this chapter – financial metrics.

GAINING INSIGHTS INTO YOUR FINANCIAL METRICS

While you may have heard of the term 'financial metrics', you may not fully understand the unique strengths and weaknesses of these metrics. As a result, if you're using them at all, you may be using financial metrics blindly, or in ways that signal misleading information. Asking yourself the questions outlined in the following sections may provide insight into your practice's financial metrics – some of which you may not have even thought about as financial metrics.

Is there more money in your account at the end of this month than there was last month?

After you pay your expenses, is the amount of cash left over in your business account increasing every month? Whether or not your cash position is getting better every month is a pretty straightforward way to measure if you're gaining profitability.

How long are your accounts receivable outstanding?

This may not be relevant for some medical businesses, and every business is different. In general, however, it's safe to say the longer you carry an overdue balance, the less profitable that balance becomes. While the length of time a practice carries an overdue balance before the profit is affected varies, healthy medical businesses have patients who pay on time.

Do you have a cash buffer?

It might be a little old fashioned, but my parents always said to live on less than I earn and put away the surplus for a rainy day. If my parents had run businesses they would have known that healthy businesses have the same attitude; it's a great idea to have money on hand to cover emergency expenses or take advantage of surprise opportunities. How much you need depends on the nature of your business, your risk tolerance and whether there is more profit in the business every month.

Setting aside money to address unforeseen expenses is a good idea – and a signifier of a healthy business.

Are your overhead expenses increasing at the same rate as your revenue?

As your business grows, your overhead expenses will probably increase – but so should your revenue. This relates back to the first question in this section. Reviewing overhead expense growth in comparison to your revenue over the course of several months might even give you an early warning sign.

How often does your inventory turn over?

The longer inventory sits on the shelf (or in the warehouse), the less profitable it becomes. When I worked at a large corporate we called it SLOB stock – Slow/Obsolete. If you pay cash for your inventory, you have money tied up that could be used somewhere else to increase profits. Shops that sell clothing, furniture and hardware feel pressure to move SLOB stock and keep their inventory turning, although they may cycle on different time frames. It is not uncommon for businesses to maintain more inventory than they really need – even medical businesses.

How often are your employees moving on?

While this isn't a financial metric, if your company is leaking employees, particularly the best employees, this should be seen as a red flag. Most employees quit their boss, not their job, and you'll commonly see a mass employee exodus when an employer ignores employees' concerns or fails to recognise employees' contributions, or an overall bad company culture exists. Every medical practice experiences turnover, but healthy practices keep happy and motivated employees.

What are your patients saying?

Every practice has a bad experience with a patient now and then. Keeping everyone happy all the time is hard. This becomes a problem when most of your patients are either complaining or seeking treatment from another doctor instead of coming back to you. If the patients are all complaining about the same issue, however, the negative feedback can be useful. Healthy practices identify, address and resolve patient concerns. While you can learn a lot from unhappy patients, healthy practices will have more happy than unhappy patients.

What does your credit profile look like?

If you want to borrow money for your practice, you should be aware of what your credit profile looks like. Business lenders will consider both your personal and business credit profile when they evaluate the health of your practice. A good credit profile is an indication of a healthy business, and it can also mean you'll likely have more loan options, better terms and better interest rates when you seek finance.

As you can see, gauging whether you have a healthy business means looking at the numbers, but other factors also need to be taken into account. Asking yourself these eight questions will provide you with high-level insight into whether your business is healthy and growing, treading water or in trouble. You can then dig deeper into problematic areas and start finding solutions. The next chapter provides more help with what perils to avoid.

8 BUSINESS TRIAGE: READY FOR GROWTH AND WHAT CAN POTENTIALLY KILL A BUSINESS?

> When everything seems to be going against you, remember that the airplane takes off against the wind, not with it.
>
> *Henry Ford*

A business structure is more pliable than a patient and, in the name of growth, you can take risks in your practice you would not take when caring for a patient. But before you throw all caution to the wind and jam your foot on the growth accelerator, you should also be aware of some known perils that can potentially destroy a business. While I encourage you to take calculated risks to evolve your practice, wielding the tools of growth can create new challenges your business may be unprepared to handle. So in this chapter, I outline the main risks that can mean death for your business.

SIX SIGNS YOU ARE READY TO EXPAND YOUR PRACTICE

> From the one who has been entrusted with much, much more will be asked.
>
> *Luke 12:48*

Taking your practice to the next stage in its development is not much different – or much easier – than launching it. It will be a combination of confidence and care that marks the doctor truly prepared to expand their practice. If you're not sure you're ready, use the following checklist to help make your decision.

You have a strong team

A strong management team that is passionate and reliable, with a great concept and lots of patient sales doesn't necessarily spell success. Expansion can put a lot of stress on your practice and, whether or not you are ready for it, will require that you give up more and more direct control. It can be a hard question for all business people, and especially professionals: are you prepared to trust your team with more decisions, and are they ready for what you're entrusting them with?

Your patients love you

Your patients can tell you a lot about whether you're ready to expand your practice. One way is by them literally telling you that you should be expanding. If you have had multiple patients asking you to open a new location or expand your services, you can be sure you have demand and a loyal patient base to rely on. Another way they can indicate you're ready for expansion is by the actions they take; for example, do patients seek you out on their own? Do they come back over and over again? These are all strong indications that your practice could well be ready for growth.

You're bursting at the seams

If demand is exceeding your capacity, you may be ready to expand soon. If the practice is becoming too cramped to breathe in, you may need to. First make sure that demand is high for many months in a row, and it's not just a spike that is temporary or dependent on something, such as a government incentive. Make sure you have the pieces of the puzzle for expansion in place before you make any decisions based solely on demand.

You have cash or finance ready

To grow you will need to make sure there is enough revenue, profit, cash flow or external finance. You may well need a lot of money to carry you through this growth phase of your expansion, and it often can involve unforeseen costs and investments that may not see returns for a long time. You should work on being profitable for a few years, so that you have sufficient cash flow to carry your practice through a successful expansion, whether or not you receive financing.

Your plans are proven

If your current success can be attributed in part to setting goals and routinely achieving them, you may be ready to take on the complex task of expanding. Reaching milestones can be a good indication that your planning skills and business model are robust and ready for new challenges. While planning for expansion, you should make sure your market's growth is favourable, and that you have a detailed marketing and sales plan for any new market you'll be expanding into.

You have systems in place

If you're not in a position to hand over the operations of your practice to someone else today – to take an extended holiday, for example – it may not be the right time for expansion. If your patient numbers doubled tomorrow, is your team ready to handle the new demand? Have you thought about where to store the extra inventory or consumables you might need? If you needed to hire three new people next week, is there a training or operations manual to guide them? Even if you do have brilliantly documented systems in place, you should know you will have to work twice as hard at the beginning of an expansion. Make sure the transition isn't any tougher for you or your team than it needs to be.

If you do not feel confident about expanding your practice right now, you should not rush. A plan for slow, organic growth is still a plan for growth. Build your team, your patient base, your profits, and your systems. Once you get to a place where you are prepared as well as excited about the challenge of expansion, you will enjoy the process much more.

POTENTIAL BUSINESS-KILLING PERILS

In this section, I describe six perils that can potentially kill a business as it moves towards growth. The perils are not listed in any order of importance and notably can, but do not necessarily, kill a business on their own. Taking note of the advance warning issued here and gaining an understanding of the dangers of growth may mean you never have to call time of death on your medical practice.

Not knowing your patients

As a medical doctor and expert health care provider, you may already feel you pay very close attention to the needs of your patients. If you do so with a mind towards innovation and the patients' ever-evolving needs, you are ahead of the game. However, despite advances in medical technology, the health care industry overall is incredibly traditional (or 'old-school'). As traditional marketplaces transition from old to new technology, numerous opportunities will emerge to adapt your practice to provide more value.

Before you launch into a new opportunity or strategy to take advantage of the changing needs of your customers, however, do some research. You should ensure you have real-time access to your data to back up your strategies. Ask yourself, how often are patients returning? How long do they spend on your webpage, or in your rooms? By gathering statistical information on your patient base, you can assess how effectively you are meeting their needs. (I delve into adapting to changing needs in more depth in chapter 19.)

Insufficient funds

The issue of not having enough money can be a symptom of fast growth, lack of planning or even success. Here's how they each affect your business:

- *Fast growth:* Rapid growth can kill a business. If you run out of capital required to support basic operational costs before your billings reach break-even point, your business will be forced to cease operations. Even if you are able to scrape together the funds to continue operating for another billing cycle, you should not necessarily feel safe, because one of many factors could disrupt the fragile balance of incoming cash and outgoing operational costs. It can be stressful because the way that cash flows in and out of your practice gets more complicated as you grow. It doesn't take much growth before your monthly expenses can exceed your operating credit, and then one bad month takes on a new meaning. Recovering from one bad month can take a long time, so watching your overheads is critical.

- *Lack of planning:* You may have underestimated the amount of cash you need to grow the practice in the way you are operating it, which may cause you to feel like you are always chasing cash. Planning as your business matures is critical to not feeling beholden to your contact at your bank.

- *Success:* While booking appointments back to back and receiving exponential increases in revenue may tempt you to increase spending, think twice and assess the business reasons for doing so. While it is true that growth requires adding team members and infrastructure, do not go on a spend-a-thon.

Not properly tracking the money you have

At times, your business may be hampered by an unexpected intervention, such as an ATO audit, unpaid work hours due to an accounting error or property damage that isn't properly insured. Keeping close track of your money is vital to guarding against financial emergencies, such as an inability to meet payroll obligations.

Making poor decisions and faulty leadership

Successful practices require motivated people. When the most driven individual in the company acts as its leader, communicating a clear and concise vision of the practice to its employees, business operations tend to run smoothly. Poor leadership can cripple a business and impede the practice from realising its potential. Growth can slow down if the leadership team loses their way or is unable to make sound decisions on the next course of action.

Aggressive competition

Pay attention to the chatter of thought leaders in your speciality. They may be privy to a new trend or process that increases the likelihood patients return. Ignoring these competitors, and their more innovative or efficient processes, may mean your medical business is left behind.

Competitors are also an excellent source of information for assessing what business strategies generate results with similar audiences. If you do not invest any time analysing the strategies of the competition or the needs of your patients, your business growth may taper off or even come to a standstill.

Distraction

Whenever a practice strays from its core market, message or mission, the results can be devastating. Maintaining focus seems like common sense, but even the most attentive and diligent practice can suffer from a sudden loss of concentration.

Lead your team with discipline, and execute on your strategic plan. If you implement a well-thought-out plan, using supporting metrics to predict success and bolster your practice's 'raison d'être', you should demonstrate your confidence in the plan by seeing it through to completion. If you are an entrepreneurial doctor, you may find (like I do) that you're uncovering so many opportunities and you want to do all of them. However, that does not do your business or your team justice. If you execute and complete a strategic plan, you might ultimately fail to obtain the results sought, but at least you will have identified the downside risk of being wrong in advance and can manage accordingly for the future.

Every business experiences a certain level of distraction from time to time. The good news is that with a little bit of leadership and foresight, you don't have to let this potential killer of businesses claim yours as its latest victim.

REASONS TO GROW YOUR PRACTICE SLOWLY

The business killing perils in the preceding section may have put you off the idea of growing your practice at all. If you did not want to grow your practice, however, you probably would not have got so far into this book. Many reasons exist to grow your practice, including economies of scale. However, some business owners who could grow their businesses instead choose to limit the growth of their enterprise.

Taking your foot off the accelerator with your practice, and focusing instead on a 'get rich slow' scheme, has many benefits. The following sections outline five of these benefits.

Time needed to achieve profitability

A practice may take a while to reach profitability, as you refine the business model. Knowing you have a profitable business model before growing is highly recommended.

Imagine if you ran a business where it cost you $7 in material and labour to make a widget that you sold for $5. No matter your sales, you're not going to make up the difference in volume. Now translate this idea to a medical business. I heard of a home health care service that routinely deployed caregivers who cost the company more in wages than the client's bill rate – that is not a business; it's a for-loss charity. It is not possible to stay in business for long with this model.

Avoidance of financial instability

When a practice is providing sufficient cash for the owner to achieve their financial objectives, many people decide not to incur the additional risk associated with further growth. Creating a lifestyle that you love could well be a focus over and above growth of the practice.

Unwillingness to let go

I have a client who loves to take care of patients, but also wants to make sure all of the practice management is taken care of by them, believing that no-one else at the office (or the world) could do it as well as they can. The size of their practice will always remain limited by their own capacity. I explain the theory of time for money earlier in this book.

Considering how comfortable you are with delegation can help you think differently about growth.

Avoidance of regulation

A practice I know of in South Australia reached a wages bill of $500,000 for services rendered. At $600,000, the business would become subject to the requirement to pay payroll tax. The practice owner decided not to cross that threshold by choice, to avoid the additional cost to the business. Certain regulatory requirements increase with growth, meaning your desire for growth can depend on your appetite for regulation.

Wish to maintain sustainable growth

In some practices, growth requires capital. When this is the case, practice owners are faced with a decision to either obtain external financing or limit growth to a rate that the business can sustain through its own internal cash generation, or through growing organically.

While you may have started reading this book thinking growth was the answer, sensible business people may have valid reasons to limit the speed at which they grow.

9 PRACTICE STRUCTURE – LET'S RUN SOME TESTS

Health is a state of complete physical, mental and social well-being, and not merely the absence of disease or infirmity.

World Health Organisation

From time to time, reflecting on the utility of your practice's business structure is a great idea from legal, compliance and risk perspectives. Putting time aside to assess your practice structure and determine whether your goals are being met by your current business model, and whether it is still the best structure available, can be time well spent for an ambitious practice owner.

You can structure a medical practice in a variety of ways, each with its advantages and disadvantages for the participating doctors and several points of view to consider, including the management of the practice as a business and each practitioner's requirements and tax considerations. You may have already received specialist structuring advice from your accounting and tax partner when you first set up the practice, but you need to ensure the structure is growing with you. Perhaps you were set up in your own business as a sole trader, but are now considering partnering with another doctor as part of your growth strategy. In this chapter, I run through the possible structures you can use when you set up your medical business, along with what you can do if you decide you need to change your structure after set-up.

For many years we have been working with a client who runs their business as a partnership of two people. The business is now a multi-million dollar operation and I shudder when I think about the risks that these two individuals are sharing together. They consider the costs of changing the structure now to be prohibitive because they own real property in the partnership and every part of their lives are intertwined. Later in this chapter I will explain the details of how a partnership operates, but the point to note here is that their business has well and truly outgrown the structure that they now feel trapped by. Consider your structuring options carefully, including how you can change them if needed.

STRUCTURING OPTIONS

The most common options and implications for structuring your medical business are outlined in the following sections. You need to understand each structure and its organisation in terms of primary function and payment of income, expenses and taxes.

Sole trader

Operating your medical practice as a sole trader is the easiest structure available to doctors. As a sole trader, you will treat patients and earn income in your own personal name, for example Dr Daisy Chain. Sole traders operate without setting up a formal business organisation, without partners, and with minimal reporting requirements. You are personally responsible for paying the tax on your income after lodging an individual (as in personal) tax return and/or business activity statements. If you welcome the lack of formalities in owning and operating your business and maintaining total control of it, being a sole trader may be your best option.

The main benefits of this type of structure are that it is simple to set up (because it's just you personally that is the entity), easy to manage and cost-effective from an accounting point of view. The main disadvantages to this type of structure are as follows:

- unlimited liability – business debts are combined with personal assets

- death of the sole proprietor means the death of the business – there is no perpetual succession

- potential lack of resources (for example, finances and skills from other experts in the business)

- limited access to finance if the business grows – you cannot raise public capital

- no flexibility in tax planning.

Medical company

A company is a separate legal entity that has the capacity to enter into contracts in its own name. Your company can be limited by shares, limited by guarantee, unlimited or a no liability company, and can be incorporated as a private company or a public company. Company shareholders enjoy limited liability, although some exceptions exist for directors.

An incorporated company that operates a medical practice receives patient fees and pays business-related expenses, with the remaining profit paid out to the doctor or doctors as a wage, plus the superannuation guarantee (like any other employee). It is not mandated that the doctor receive all the profit. An incorporated company is required to register and pay workers compensation insurance, as well as pay employee PAYG tax payments to the Australian Taxation Office. You should be aware that incorporating a company to run your medical practice does not protect you against patient litigation (the reason you carry insurance).

Even though people use the term 'company' in a way that suggests only one type is possible, different kinds of companies and structures exist – including public or proprietary, no liability companies or unlimited with share capital. So what is the difference between a company limited by shares versus by a guarantee? The following is a very short summary.

Company limited by shares

A company limited by shares is one of the most popular separate legal entities used by businesses in Australia today. A company limited by shares is a company in which the liability of its members (also known as shareholders) is limited to the amount (if any) unpaid on the shares held by them.

Shareholders of companies limited by shares have limited liability. The directors of a company limited by shares are also not liable for the debts of the company. However, they can become personally liable if they engage in activities contrary to their legal obligations, or if they enter into personal guarantees for the company's obligations. This is covered in more detail in my first book, *How to Avoid A Fall from Grace: Legal Lessons for Directors*.

This may be slightly more information than you need about companies, but a company limited by shares can be either a public or a proprietary (private) company. So, what's the difference? Well, firstly it's the number of shareholders that they can have – a proprietary company cannot have more than 50 non-employee shareholders. Secondly, it has a restricted right to transfer shares and it is not able to undertake any commercial activities (except in limited circumstances) that would require disclosure under Section 6D of the *Corporations Act 2001* (Cth).

A proprietary company may be large or small. The size is a calculation of their assets and revenue as well as the number of entities in the company's group, or in other words that the company controls. Small proprietary companies have fewer reporting requirements.

A public company can issue securities to the public, and has greater disclosure and reporting requirements than a proprietary company.

A requirement of all companies limited by shares is that they must include the term 'limited' in their name to alert potential creditors that the company has limited liability.

Company limited by guarantee

A company limited by guarantee is a public company that limits its members' liability to the amount that each member undertakes to contribute to the business's property if (and when) it is wound up. A guarantee in this context will be for a fixed amount.

A company limited by guarantee cannot issue shares, and its members do not receive dividends from profits. It does not have share capital and is not able to raise equity. Businesses do not typically run as companies limited by guarantee, but they are common among the not-for-profit or charity sector.

Director's duties

My first book, *How to Avoid a Fall from Grace: Legal Lessons for Directors*, is a great book to read if you are or are going to become a director of a company. (I also call it a 'Guidebook to Navigating the Modern Corporate World'.) As the leader of a company, you have a lot to worry about on a daily basis. The last thing you need to invest your time in is agonising over the complex legal issues that underpin your actions. The book offers advice gathered from more than a decade of working with Australian and international companies of every shape and size.

Advantages and disadvantages of companies

The company tax imputation system prevents taxing at the shareholder and company level. Contributions made by your company to a superannuation fund on behalf of employees can be claimed by the company as a tax deduction. If you are in a group of companies, any losses can be transferred from one company to another in the group, provided full common ownership is in place. Your company tax rate is set at a much lower rate than the highest individual tax rate. After your death or retirement, the company will continue. Issuing new shares in the company is quite easy as is bringing in new ownership without creating a new entity.

The disadvantages of operating as a medical company are as follows:

* some establishment costs
* ongoing maintenance costs such as annual filing fees and accounting fees (generally, greater accountability means increased complexity and costs)

- onerous compliance tasks governed by ASIC rules and the Corporations Act
- negative gearing results in the trapping of tax losses within the company
- ineligibility for the capital gains tax (CGT) 50 per cent discount concession (this is available to individuals and superannuation funds).

Discretionary trust

In a discretionary trust (also known as a family trust) the beneficiaries do not have a fixed entitlement or interest in the trust funds. It can be set up to receive income (via patient billings and Medicare) and pay business expenses, with the profits being paid as doctor's wages or trust distributions.

Service business

A service business is a separate entity (in most cases a company) that is incorporated to provide administrative support. How does it work? Usually, the practice will receive patient fee income and Medicare funds and pay expenses (such as doctor's wages, superannuation, PI insurance, registrations and so on) while the service business will receive a service fee and pay expenses such as practice costs, lease costs, equipment, and other wages. The service entity may earn a small profit that can be split with related parties (such as non-doctor spouses). The key benefit of using a service business is that it is flexible and provides asset protection by isolating business risks from the individual doctor.

(I am not a tax expert, but speaking to your accountant about how the Personal Services Tax laws will apply to your structure is a great idea; it's something I have personally been caught out by before.)

Partnership

A partnership structure involves two or more persons operating a business in common with a view to profit. It is relatively inexpensive to establish and can be informally agreed to by the parties' conduct, although I always recommend having a partnership agreement. The legislative regulation for partnerships is relatively minimal, and partners are not required to make public disclosures. Partners can, in fact, regulate themselves and resolve problems together.

Tax losses can be used immediately by the partners against income from other sources. This is useful during start-up, when a business often loses money, because partners can deduct losses from their personal income. The partnership can be set up to vary profits or losses between partners on an annual basis. Partners hold an interest in each partnership asset as an individual and so are able to access the 50 per cent CGT discount.

The disadvantages of operating a partnership are as follows:

- partnership may exist 'at law' (the business may be deemed a legal partnership due to the partners' behaviour), even if that was not the plan

- unlimited liability – the partners are all jointly and severally liable for the debts of the practice

- partnership agreements must be amended to add or remove partners

- transferring a partner's personal share in the partnership is difficult

- taxable income flows through to partners, so partners pay higher tax rates when the business makes money

- the maximum number of partners is set at 20, which may restrict growth

- partnership Acts vary from state to state, which may hinder interstate partnerships

- one partner's actions can bind the other partners

- partners hold interests in each partnership asset as individuals.

The final point in the preceding lists means that, if a partnership asset is sold, each partner is treated as having disposed of an asset for CGT purposes, as represented by that partner's percentage interest.

Joint venture

When individuals enter into a business relationship for a specific purpose, the structure is known as a joint venture. Joint ventures may be incorporated or unincorporated. As always, it is always preferable to enter into a written agreement that memorialises the parties' expectations, conduct and vision for the venture. Negotiating contract terms forces the parties to think about the purpose and goals of the venture, as well as the rights and obligations of the parties when a specified event occurs. Reducing an agreement to writing can save all parties a fortune when the outcome of the venture is uncertain. Participants in a joint venture are not usually responsible for the acts of other participants.

An example of a joint venture is the website Whitecoat, which was established by the private health insurer NIB to provide non-clinical reviews of health care providers such as dentists and physiotherapists. The service was expanded to a joint venture with health funds Bupa and HBF to cover doctors and specialists, with reviews and a guide to gap fees. The website now describes itself as 'TripAdvisor for health care'.

Unless stated otherwise, each participant may transfer or assign his/her rights without the consent of the other participants in areas not relating to the joint venture.

The disadvantages of a joint venture are as follows:

- lack of longevity, because a joint venture exists only as long as contemplated to reach a specified goal and may terminate if one participant retires, unless reconstituted with new members

- venturers are liable for the debts of the venture on a joint and several basis

- expanded operations of the business venture are restricted, and the agreement would need to be amended to proceed with other related business ideas

- limitations on transferability – a joint venture cannot be sold intact and must be liquidated for sale.

Each structure attracts different associated risks and tax consequences, and what is right for your practice will depend on your personal circumstances – that's one of the reasons that lawyers often say 'it depends' when you ask a question. For specific advice relating to your medical business, talk with your accountant or financial planner.

Entering a partnership or joint venture as a company

Entering into an arrangement that you might think of as a 'joint venture' or a 'partnership' as a company limited by shares is possible. If you and your business partner(s) incorporate a new company, you can divide the ownership by the shareholding and document the arrangement in a shareholder's agreement. This manages risk, by keeping the business enterprise in a separate legal entity, and manages succession because you can agree beforehand on a method to use to value the company in the event that one of you no longer wants to be involved with the business. You can own the shares in the company in an entity you choose – whether that is personally or in another company or a trust. I recommend being guided by your tax advisor on this particular aspect of the structuring.

CHANGING YOUR BUSINESS STRUCTURE ONCE YOUR PRACTICE IS OPERATING

When you first started out working as a doctor, you may have been an employee in your own name. As you moved to start your own business or work as a consultant you may have started with a sole trader structure and then either moved or be moving to a company structure because either you or your accountant feels the time is right to move to the more tax-efficient, safer company structure. The following sections set out the steps to take to move your business structure from sole trader to company quickly, efficiently and, as much as is possible, in a cost-effective manner.

Decide on ownership and office holders

Will you be bringing on board new shareholders or not? If you are, work out if you're going to have more than one office holder or not – that is, will you be the sole director/secretary or will you share the responsibility with others? Once you have chosen you will be in a position to incorporate your company.

Incorporate

Depending on where you are at with your practice, you may have realised that a 'Pty Ltd' company is very popular for medical practitioners. An accountant or lawyer can assist with this, and also counsel you on whether it is worthwhile using a trust as well. Choosing a company name can be fun, but you may not choose a company name that is being used by someone else. You may wish to name the company the same name as the business name you've been trading under as a sole trader. Be aware that simply registering a company name does not protect the intellectual property within your business – read chapter 11 to find out more on this topic.

Update business documents

There will be business documents that you need to amend once the new structure is in place; for example, your business terms and conditions will need to be amended, your business cards, your letterhead and your website will also need updating. It's likely that the changes will be relatively minor, but your terms and other business documents must reflect the fact that the business entity has changed.

Advise your patients and suppliers

Patients and suppliers may need to be informed that you're now trading through a company. Some stakeholders may need to be advised of your new bank account details (and your new business terms and conditions). If you're operating under contractual arrangements with any patients or suppliers, you may need to cancel or assign the existing contracts, with your company as the counterparty to any legal documents. I recommend doing this as quickly and efficiently as possible to minimise any hassle for your accountant.

Inform your insurance provider

This one is really important: remember to update your insurance provider that you're now operating through a company so that you remain properly insured.

Transfer employment contracts

Employees or contractors you have will need to be transferred to the new company.

Transfer assets to the company

The final step will be transferring assets, and it is the most complicated. Many sole trader doctors don't actually have many assets. If you do need to transfer assets it's important to discuss the transaction with your accountant or a tax lawyer. The tax treatment of the transfer is crucial to ensure that you make the transfers as tax-effective as possible.

You may have gathered by reading this chapter that changing your business structure can be quite complex; good legal advice in order to avoid legal or tax issues in the future is important if you need to change your structure.

10 DOCUMENTING WHAT HAS BEEN AGREED: SHAREHOLDERS' AGREEMENTS

Mutual respect is the foundation of genuine harmony.

Dalai Lama

If you are going into business with another doctor, the partnership or joint venture options discussed in the preceding chapter may be of particular interest to you. Indeed, as also covered in chapter 9, entering into a partnership or joint venture as a company is a great way to manage risk and succession. However, entering into such structures creates the need for a shareholders' agreement to be drafted, and I receive many questions about these agreements from medical professionals. Due to the volume of requests for clarification that I receive, including a whole chapter on shareholders' agreements seemed prudent. The challenge was writing about corporate law in a way that holds your attention.

Yes, *of course* a commercial lawyer wants smart doctors to enter into (and understand) the terms of a shareholders' agreement. But I haven't always been a commercial lawyer – I used to work in commercial litigation. In the law, we refer to the setting up phase of a business and its operational side (before anything goes wrong) as the 'front end'; commercial litigation, on the other hand, is known as the 'back end' (the puns on this could abound). I worked in commercial litigation at the beginning of my career and, in particular, I worked in bankruptcy and insolvency. In my experience, the death of countless businesses can be attributed to shareholders who failed to consider the many potential events that could go wrong in their business and lacked a simple procedure for resolving disputes among shareholders.

A shareholders' agreement governs the shareholders' expectations, conduct and vision for the business by describing how the company should operate, and identifying the shareholders' rights and obligations. Shareholders' agreements, however, cannot provide guidance for every possible scenario that may impact a business. Further, due to cognitive biases, two logical shareholders may perceive the same event differently and, thus, disagree on how the business should respond to it.

The proverbial question, 'Is the glass half full or half empty?' demonstrates how an object may be perceived in two different, but equally rational, ways, depending on one's point of view. Similarly, cognitive biases can cause individuals to perceive different levels of risk posed by the same event. Where one shareholder sees the opportunity presented by an event ('the glass is half full'), another shareholder may see only danger ('the glass is half empty').

In this book's introduction, I mentioned that, to me, doctors and lawyers share many professional characteristics. Risk consciousness is a professional trait exhibited in both the medical and legal fields. Doctors and attorneys examine not only the steps necessary to accomplish a goal, but also alternative methods for reaching the same goal. They then assess the risks posed by each alternative. A risk-conscious mindset prioritises reducing risk over increasing opportunity ('the glass is half empty' mindset). Risk aversion is exhibited by professionals who desire to protect the wellbeing of the clients or patients. In other words, the professional preference for risk aversion arises from the closeness of the attorney–client and/or doctor–patient relationship and illustrates the extent to which the professional decision-making process is influenced by the stakes to clients or patients. This means risk aversion tendencies result from an effort to reduce the stakes for the client or patient.

From a lawyer's perspective, the stakes usually involve a client's financial condition but, in the case of a criminal lawyer, may involve higher stakes such as the liberty (and sometimes, the life) of the client. It is easy to understand why doctors develop a risk-averse mindset on behalf of patients and their families. Indeed, the burden of making decisions with such potentially high-stakes consequences is often associated with high stress and emotional or substance abuse issues in this profession.

However, as a factor in business growth, and in the context of structuring a medical practice, risk is treated much differently. The shareholders' agreement, through attempting to capture the shareholders' expectations, conduct and vision for the business, also attempts to capture their attitudes to practice and business risk.

KNOWING WHAT TO INCLUDE IN THE AGREEMENT

So, if smart doctors need a shareholders' agreement, what terms should be included in it? How should doctors manage practice risks as shareholders? Can the risk-conscious mindset, vital to protecting the wellbeing of patients, infect a shareholders' agreement to frustrate business growth?

A shareholders' agreement for a medical practice is a contract between each shareholder of a company. It operates differently from a constitution in that it governs the relationship between shareholders by setting out their rights and responsibilities with each other. The specific purpose of the shareholders' agreement is to outline how the shareholders should act (or remind them how they have agreed to act) when certain events occur.

A company constitution, on the other hand, is a document that generally specifies the rules governing the relationship between, and the activities of, the company, its directors and shareholders.

A company's constitution is essentially a contract between the company and each shareholder, a shareholder and each other shareholder, and the company and each director and company secretary, under which each person (or entity, depending on how the shares are held) agrees to observe the provisions of the constitution so far as they apply to that person (or entity). This creates enforceable rights and obligations in relation to shareholders in their capacity as shareholders of the company, not in their personal capacity.

The *Corporations Act 2001* (Cth) sets out some fundamental shareholder rights, such as requiring a majority vote to change the share structure, but many additional strategic considerations, operational decisions and risk management factors can, and should, be addressed in a shareholders' agreement, particularly for medical practices.

We often hear of medical 'partnerships', but given the unique risks faced by medical practitioners, a true partnership is a rare and ill-advised structure for physicians. A shareholders' agreement, however, will unite the shareholders of a corporate practice, allowing them to set the parameters for management and board composition, valuation, buy-ins and income distribution, in much the same way as a partnership.

Remember – a partnership is ill-advised because it is defined as two people working together in common business. A partnership is not a separate legal entity; instead, it is two parties together in business (and this often in their own personal names). Then the income and the expenses of the venture is collated and then split equally between the parties. The parties then report this income in their own right, making it not a very popular method of business in modern times.

The following categories should be considered for inclusion when drafting a shareholders' agreement.

Management and decision-making

Your shareholders' agreement should set out strategic management decisions of the practice, including provisions regarding composition of the board and appointment of and removal of directors.

The largest portion of your agreement will most likely be dedicated to explaining how the practice will be managed, and the procedure for decision-making. You can specify whether decisions will require a majority vote (that is, 50 per cent), special resolution (75 per cent) or unanimous vote (100 per cent) of approval. Or you may decide to stipulate that specific decisions cannot be made without 100 per cent shareholder approval.

Dividends and financing

Your shareholders' agreement will prescribe the conditions for dividend payments. It may also set out rights and obligations of shareholders with respect to additional funding, shareholder and director loans, and other circumstances under which the company may enter into debt arrangements.

Exit strategy

The most common questions I hear about shareholders' agreements involve exit strategies and unexpected exits by a shareholder due to illness, injury or death. Here I cover how this relates to the shareholders' agreement – I will go more into personal succession planning in chapter 21, so stay tuned for that.

When a fellow shareholder wants to exit the practice, the shareholder can be required to offer their shares to existing shareholders at a specified price. This can prevent a situation where shares are sold or transferred to someone who is incompatible with the practice. The agreement should also detail how a valuation of equity should be calculated, and how any shared assets, such as medical equipment, will be valued.

In the event of the death of a shareholder, you can include provisions to either ensure the shares are offered to existing shareholders or permit the company to buy back the shares. Buy-backs in these circumstances can sometimes force the company into a cash flow problem, as it tries to secure funds to pay the deceased estate. To avoid this issue, most shareholders' agreements construct a buy-back that occurs over time. In some circumstances, providing in the agreement that shares are purchased using the proceeds of a life insurance policy might be appropriate.

Funding contributions

The most common funding for shareholder buy-ins are cash contributions. You may, however, want to include a provision in your shareholders' agreement to define the circumstances in which shareholders can buy in with 'sweat equity'; that is, the conditions under which individuals who have worked for the practice for several years may acquire shares in the company.

Dispute resolution

Two of the biggest advantages of drafting a shareholders' agreement are, firstly, the certainty it provides and, secondly, the actual process of discussing concerns openly with your practice partners as you draft the agreement reduces the risk of disputes in the long term. That being said, any shareholders' agreement worth its salt will also set out the process of mediation and/or arbitration in the event a dispute does arise.

As always, if you have any questions about what should be in your shareholders' agreement and how it should be phrased, talk with your lawyer.

In appendix B I have included as a checklist some of the key areas that may be considered by you when drafting a Shareholder's Agreement.

11 YOUR INTELLECTUAL PROPERTY IS A BUSINESS ASSET

The patent system added fuel of interest to the fire of genius.

Abraham Lincoln

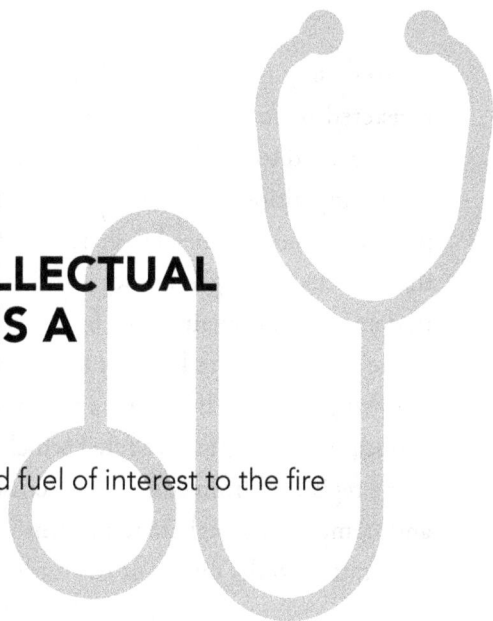

As a practice owner, you may not have thought much about protecting your intellectual property. Don't worry – you are not alone. Many business owners forget to address intellectual property as a business asset. In this chapter, I take you through what intellectual property actually is, and how to enforce your rights in the case of any infringements.

UNDERSTANDING WHAT'S INCLUDED
What is considered intellectual property? The phrase relates to property including copyrighted works, patents, trademarks and trade secrets. With so many other legal considerations to consider in the operation of a medical practice, doctors do not often consider their intellectual property rights until there has been an infringement. Understanding what actually is included is the first step to being aware of how you might protect these assets.

Domain names
If you intend on registering a domain name for your medical practice but have found out the domain name you want and most common domain

suffixes using this name (such as 'com' and 'com.au') have already been registered to someone else, do not despair. Additional domain suffixes (also referred to as a 'top-level domain') are now available.

Competition to register a domain name can involve intellectual property issues that need to be resolved in litigation. You should be aware that 'cybersquatting' is not legal and occurs when an individual registers a trademark as a domain name for the purpose of selling the domain name to the actual trademark owner for a profit. (Trademarks are covered in the following section.) If you are a victim of cybersquatting, you may file an application for injunctive relief which, if granted, prohibits the domain name registrant from continuing to use the trademark as a domain name and compels the registrant to transfer ownership of the domain name registration to the owner of the trademark.

The international Uniform Domain Name Dispute Resolution Policy (UDRP) sets forth the rules applicable to the resolution of disputes over domain name registrations, including claims of abusive and/or bad faith registration, and mandates the parties' participation in a nonbinding, low-cost administrative proceeding.

Trademarks

Medical professionals who use symbols, logos, slogans or other identifying 'marks' to identify their medical services or products in 'trade' (such as advertising or promotional materials) may establish the right to register a 'trademark'. Even particular colours can be part of your trademark. A trademark, whether registered or unregistered, is owned by you, but registering a trademark provides the owner with an exclusive right to use the mark in the specific class you register it in.

A trademark is a powerful marketing device (making up a big part of what is known as a 'brand') that facilitates consumer recognition. A trademark can be used as either a shield or a sword. Registering your trademark gives you superior rights to the trademark and protects ('shields') your use of all aspects that make up the trademark from an infringement lawsuit. You can also wield a registered trademark as a sword in your practice to stop a competitor from using the elements within it to benefit from your goodwill and reputation and/or dilute your trademark's value. A trademark can lose value when consumers become confused about what services or products are represented by a certain trademark (and so business) and begin associating it with a competitor's inferior services or goods.

A registered trademark is an investment for your practice. If one day you decide to sell your practice, a trademark with substantial consumer recognition adds value to a business sale. An established brand with a registered trademark is more attractive to potential buyers than an unregistered mark.

Patents

Patents are the most misunderstood element of intellectual property. A patent grants the owner the commercial rights to any device, substance, method or process they have created that is new, inventive and useful. Australia recognises two types of patents: standard and innovation.

Patents relevant to doctors are pharmaceutical and medical technologies patents. The Australian Patent Office grants patents for methods of medical treatment, including new surgical procedures, while the European Patent Office does not. Australian patents can be used to protect against infringement by a wide variety of potential infringers, including hospitals, suppliers, manufacturers and professional service providers.

As the inventor, you may believe you are the most knowledgeable person to draft a patent application, and you may think it is a clever way to save money. Please do not do this. The patent approval process is so technical that even lawyers must have special qualifications to represent inventors applying for patents. Preparation of a patent application itself is a very complex task governed by a series of convoluted laws, rules and customs. Therefore, inventors who independently prepare and represent themselves during the patent application process oftentimes spend more money than they would have if they had hired a patent attorney from the outset. It is not an uncommon occurrence for inventors to hire patent attorneys to repair a self-prepared patent application in response to an office action (see my note above saying not to do your own patent application – this is why). If the patent attorney can't correct the application the inventor may lose the 'priority' of his or her filing date or potentially the ability to patent the invention altogether.

Recent patenting innovations

In the medical industry the innovations that are being patented are ground-breaking, and moving so quickly that the innovations I've listed here potentially won't be seen as revolutionary for long. Hopefully, they can still give you an idea of the kinds of innovations that can be patented. Some recent highlights include:

- *Virtual reality diagnosis and recovery:* Sophisticated devices like the Oculus Rift have hit the market and medical students have started examining patients through VR.

- *Handheld ultrasound:* Ultrasound machines are now pocket-size – and they're getting smaller. It's expected that pocket-sized visualisation tools may replace the humble stethoscope (which could render the cover of this book redundant).

- *Real-time food scanners:* Instead of attempting to guess the nutritional value of your food, a scanner is now available that uses near-infrared spectroscopy to determine the chemical makeup of food and drink. After a scan of about 10 seconds, a nutritional breakdown appears on the accompanying app and, from there, you can determine how what you're about to eat may fit into a predetermined diet or wellness plan.

- *An augmented reality lens:* A digital contact lens that can monitor blood sugar for people with diabetes has been developed. The chip and sensor are embedded between two layers of contact lens material and a tiny pinhole allows fluid from the eye to reach the glucose sensor, measuring levels every second. The contact lens will allow people with diabetes to check glucose more often and more easily than the current method of pricking their finger.

- *Organ bioprinting:* For the first time, fully-human kidney proximal tubular tissues have been generated that are three-dimensional, and made up of multiple tissue-relevant cell types arranged to copy the renal tube functions.

- *Immediate test results:* Point-of-care testing (PoCT) is pathology testing performed at the time of consultation that allows the results to be used to make immediate, informed decisions about patient care.

Trade secrets

Trade secrets are defined as a formula, process, recipe or method that is not generally known or ascertainable by the public. The most famous unknown trade secret in the world is the recipe for Coca-Cola.

While not technically 'intellectual property', your patient list is a business asset best described as a trade secret.

Under Australian law, trade secrets are granted protection under the equitable principles of Confidential Information. We treat things like patient lists and other trade secrets as confidential information because doing so can offer far greater legal protection than copyright provisions, particularly against unauthorised use or disclosure, rather than the limited protections, such as prohibiting reproduction, afforded under copyright.

Whether something will be considered a trade secret is determined by several factors, such as:

- whether the information is sensitive or has the necessary quality of confidence
- what steps you have taken to protect the information, such as limited access or non-disclosure agreements
- the value of the information you are protecting.

Customer lists in a regular retail business, for example, might be considered know-how, but are not granted the same level of protection as a recognised trade secret. Patient lists, on the other hand, could be described as so confidential in nature that a reasonable person would consider it unconscionable to steal, copy or trade them.

In addition to registering any intellectual property, such as patents and trademarks, you should also ensure that you take steps to protect your patient lists and any other trade secrets.

The most effective way of doing this is to make sure that you have effective non-disclosure and confidentiality documents in place with your employees, contractors and anyone else who may have access to your patient lists.

'Restraint of trade' clauses can also be valuable if you are trying to prevent employees from using trade secrets or know-how following termination of employment. It should be noted, however, that restraint of trade clauses are fickle and infamously difficult to enforce. They should be drafted very carefully and I recommend engaging an employment lawyer to do so.

This is a big discussion point for employed doctors. You may have noticed that employers are now regularly including restraint of trade clauses in employment contracts to protect their practice when former employees or contractors begin working for a competitor. These restraints of trade can be included in employment contracts and also contractor agreements to protect an employer's trade secrets, confidential information, patient details and team member connections by restricting an employee's or contractor's activities after they have left the practice. The contractual issue with restraint of trade clauses is that they will only be enforceable to the extent that the restraint is 'reasonably necessary' to protect the legitimate business interests of the employer. Whether a clause is 'reasonably necessary' will depend on the particular clause and circumstances.

Copyright

Copyright could potentially cover many assets created by your practice, so it's wise to have a general understanding of it. Copyright is simply but broadly defined as a bundle of rights that attach to certain creative works such as text, visual artistic works, computer programs, sound recordings and films. A copyright owner acquires an exclusive right to reproduce the copyrighted material or perform or show the work to the public. Copyright owners can prevent others from reproducing, communicating or displaying their work without permission, and may sell or licence these rights to someone else.

In Australia, to obtain the copyright to creative material, the owner does not need to register the material. Copyright protection is acquired automatically, as a matter of law, as soon as the materials are produced or take on a material form. This usually occurs when an idea is written down or recorded in either visual or auditory form.

When your practice creates copyrighted material (such as pamphlets, an operations manual, photographs and/or video taken of your practice's products or services, and even the content of your practice's website), you own the copyright to that material and must enforce those rights to prevent any claims to the material or misuse by third parties in the future.

ENFORCING INTELLECTUAL PROPERTY RIGHTS IN A TIMELY MANNER

Establishing your rights as the owner of a trademark, patent or copyrighted material is only the first step in protecting your intellectual property rights. It is your responsibility as the owner of the intellectual property to protect it from infringement by others. There is no IP police, so to speak, and the law requires you to enforce your own intellectual property rights.

Failure to take affirmative action to protect your intellectual property within a reasonable time may result in substantial loss to the practice. A trademark can also become generic through overuse and lose its protection altogether. There is a time limit on the enforcement of intellectual property rights, so note you may be barred by a statute of limitations if you wait too long. If you do wait too long, the infringer may be able to raise equitable defences such as waiver and abandonment.

To avoid this issue, your practice should establish a procedure for identifying and taking appropriate action to stop any infringement of your intellectual property. One option involves employing a professional 'watch' organisation. Another option is asking your team, family, patients and friends to alert you when they discover materials that potentially infringe on your intellectual property rights. If a potential infringement is identified, doctors should immediately consult with an intellectual property lawyer and issue cease-and-desist letters to the infringers as early as possible. If the demand letter is ineffective, additional steps can be taken to protect and enforce your rights. Your intellectual property is an asset that can be leveraged. Taking care of it at the outset will pay off in the long run.

PART IV

OPERATIONS DON'T JUST HAPPEN IN THEATRE

You may not appreciate the presence of good health but you will definitely regret the absence of good health, because health is happiness.

Amit Kalantri

The classroom education taught in medical school lays a necessary foundation for the clinical, practical and specialty training learned by medical interns and residents. Your continuing growth as a medical practitioner requires you stay current with new medical procedures and technologies. Similarly, the evolution from private practice doctor to private practice business innovator and grower requires more from you, as owner of the business, than just managing income, expenses and employees.

In part III, we learned the importance of examining business structures and practices to determine business health and considered whether implementing change could enable you to more quickly or efficiently reach your practice goals (or could kill the business). Thus far in this book, I have encouraged you to analyse your practice in conjunction with your goals. Thinking about your business, however, does not effectuate change. Like I always say (I can't believe I wrote that sentence), thinking about something does not translate to action in the real world.

Now it's time to operate. Now that you've assessed your business structure, practices and general health, you may be ready to implement some changes. I am eager to give you some practical legal tips on how to improve the operations side of your business.

12 LEASE, LICENCE OR LANDLORD: LEGAL LESSONS IN BRICKS AND MORTAR

May your choices reflect your hopes. Not your fears.

Nelson Mandela

One of the most important decisions you will make prior to opening your medical practice involves 'bricks and mortar' – that is, where patients will go to receive your services. In addition to selecting a geographic location, building/office style and interior decor, you must also decide what financial arrangement you will use to secure your exclusive use of the office space. Your options include:

- leasing property
- purchasing property
- licencing property to occupy.

In this book, I've assumed you are currently operating your own medical practice and, accordingly, have already entered into one of the financial arrangements discussed in this chapter. However, as your practice grows and matures, you may need to reassess whether your current arrangement aligns with your practice's structure and goals. Understanding the legal issues raised by each option will help you determine whether a change is necessary or, if you are considering relocating your practice, will prepare you for selecting the most appropriate financial arrangement for your business.

LEASE YOUR OFFICE

Location, location, location. Finding property to lease is a popular and simple way of securing the space to operate your business. A commercial property lessor invests the capital and absorbs the risk in owning the property your practice will call 'home'. Whether you lease space in an existing medical precinct or select a location that is ideal for other reasons (for example, high demand, great parking or next door to a pharmacy), your choice will reflect the needs of your specialty and business model.

For most practice owners, the most important term in a lease is the amount of rent charged and rent escalations. Your options may be determined by your budget and business model but, as a colleague recently noted, in the grand scheme of expenses incurred to set up and operate a business, rent is cheap compared to the cost of hiring people.

While considering the terms relevant to the rent, rent escalations, the lease and option clauses is important, clauses unique to commercial leases can have a substantial negative affect on your rights and responsibilities as a tenant. If you do not learn to recognise these terms (or delegate this task to someone else on your team or your lawyer), you can incur significant unexpected costs by unwittingly assuming obligations and risks above and beyond market practice or what a landlord may reasonably require.

Remember – option clauses can be (and usually are) advantageous to both parties in a commercial lease. They are fairly standard in most commercial lease agreements. What is an 'option'? An option is a term in a lease agreement that permits a tenant, upon meeting certain conditions, to have the term of the lease renewed for a pre-agreed period.

An option can be referred to as a 'further term' or 'lease renewal', but in exercising an option, you are entering into a completely new lease with the landlord that is binding, and enforceable by both parties.

Until the deed of renewal or new lease has been created and signed by both parties, there is only an agreement to lease. I recommend having an expert draft these documents after (if not before) the notice to exercise the option has been delivered to the landlord.

Some of the hidden risks, opportunities and issues you should consider when prospecting commercial property as a tenant are covered in the following sections.

Lease incentives and 'face rent'

Lease incentives can very much depend on the state of the rental market; for example, a landlord may offer an initial incentive to a tenant to take on a lease, such as a fit-out allowance or reduced rent for an introductory period. These incentives are always recouped throughout the balance of the term by an inflated rent (the 'face rent'), so that the commercial outcome for you as a tenant is the equivalent of what you would have paid using a simpler rental structure.

This structure could simply be the product of a landlord's internal preferences, and it may appear to be a fantastic opportunity for you to keep some extra cash on hand while you build your practice, but buyer beware – 'face rent' structures can, and often do, include some tricky clauses with unexpected consequences.

Market rent reviews

I mentioned the 'face rent' risk, but market rent review clauses should also be treated with caution.

'Market rent' can be set at whatever rent the landlord nominates, and then the tenant is deemed to automatically accept the landlord's rental figure, unless the tenant proactively challenges it within a specified period. An unanticipated (and undesirable) result of such a clause is that a simple administrative oversight can lock the tenant into an additional lease term with unreasonably high rent.

Make-good and general repair obligations

Make-good and general repair clauses will likely already be familiar to you, because they are commonly included in both residential tenancy and commercial leases and, for the most part, meet standard practice expectations. (In case you're unsure, a make-good clause basically requires you to return the property to its original state when vacating.)

You need to, however, watch out for a few things when reviewing make-good and general repair obligations. These include the following:

- *Tenant deemed to be 'holding over' upon failure to satisfy 'make-good' obligations:* 'Holding over' is a term used to describe the legal status of a tenant who retains possession of the property after termination of the lease, and without consent of the landlord. A landlord may include a clause in the lease that provides the tenant is 'deemed' to be 'holding over' (thus obligating the tenant to pay rent under the rationale that a tenant 'holding over' retains possession of the property without consent) when a tenant has vacated the premises but has failed to fully comply with make-good obligations. Depending on the precise wording of a make-good clause, a clause that deems a tenant to be 'holding over' when the tenant fails to fully comply with immaterial make-good obligations may allow an unscrupulous landlord to strictly enforce the two clauses and so continue to charge the departed tenant full rent while the landlord finds a replacement tenant.

- *Conflict with subletting provisions:* I have had a client that has been caught out by subletting premises for the balance of a lease term. In doing so they were left with insufficient time, at the end of the sublease, to comply with – in their case – significant make-good obligations before the end of the lease term.

- *Structural soundness and weatherproofing:* Most standard commercial leases do not require landlords to keep the building structurally sound and weatherproofed. I have had a client that ran a professional services business, and the roof of their office building leaked every time it rained. It caused significant angst to the owner of the business, as you can imagine. In the absence of an obligation like this, circumstances (like the one I have just described) can arise that make it very difficult for the tenant to comply with general repair obligations.

Risk of disputes

Which party is responsible for repairing or maintaining the premises is determined through interpreting the terms of the lease. This may sound simple, but, what is meant by 'maintenance' and 'repair' and sometimes what is 'structural' can be a matter of interpretation. Paying attention to these definitions is important, because they're the cause of the majority of disputes that arise between landlords and tenants.

'Structural repairs' can include repairs to the building support system or foundations, walls and, depending on the lease and the building in question, may also include the roof.

A 'repair' can be defined as doing the necessary work to fix something that has been damaged. It may have been accidentally damaged or damaged as a result of continued use. If a tenant themselves or visitors damage part of the premises, the tenant is always responsible for the repairs. Questions can arise when an item, such as a latch on a door that is used frequently, wears out and requires repair – the parties may not agree about who should fix it.

The landlord may say that the latch was damaged due to the tenant's lack of care or proper or regular maintenance, and the tenant may say that it was faulty or had reached the end of its useful life. Disputes may arise which then cost the parties time and money, so it is best to ensure that the lease is specific and clear in the areas where the potential for disagreement exists. Even though you may be excited about getting into the new premises sooner rather than later, taking the time to make sure that the lease is reviewed will be an excellent investment in your business and also for your peace of mind.

'Maintenance' is considered to be the taking of some action to delay wear and tear or deterioration or breakage of an item – for example, cleaning and servicing of plant and equipment or proper disposal of waste and garbage.

A lease may outline that the tenant should clear the drains, for example, and then if there is a plumbing issue, the landlord may say that the reason the drains failed was that the tenant did not do the maintenance required by the lease. In response, the tenant may say that the plumbing was old and needed updating. You can see in this example how easily a dispute can be created about who is to fix the costly plumbing problem.

A sensible starting point for both the tenant and the landlord that can lessen the likelihood of dispute is having an independent third party undertake a full inspection report of the premises, with both parties signing off on the report. This will establish and document what condition the premises was in prior to entry of the tenant.

It is in your interests if you are a landlord or a tenant to ensure that a commercial lease contains clear obligations and well-defined standards for the repair and maintenance of the property, to reduce the risk of a dispute and misunderstanding between the parties.

Hopefully you can see through reading this section of the book that the law is not always clear in this area, particularly when it comes to repair and maintenance obligations. It can be the case that even where there is legislation which says that a repair is the landlord's obligation, the lease (usually written by the landlord) can change this and make the tenant responsible. I highly recommend that each party should, therefore, ensure that they receive their own legal advice to ensure their best interests are protected in the lease.

Indemnities for loss or damage beyond tenant's control

A standard clause included in commercial leases obligates a tenant to indemnify the landlord against certain losses – for example, where the tenant fails to comply with their obligation to repair damage to the property, the tenant must compensate the landlord for the cost of the repairs the tenant failed to make, as well as any additional damages immediately caused by the tenant's failure to repair.

Indemnity obligations that raise a red flag are a tenant's obligation to indemnify the landlord for damages caused by factors outside the tenant's control. An example of such damages would be damages caused by the tenant's guests or clients when they were leaving the property (for example, the tenant's visitors drove over the landlord's prize-winning rose bushes planted at the entrance to the parking lot adjacent to the tenant's leased premises). In this example, the tenant should not be required to indemnify the landlord for the cost of replacing the rose bushes regardless of the degree of control the tenant had over his guests or clients while they were on the leased premises.

Not only is it impossible to manage risks outside of your control, but a medical practice tenant assuming liability for such risks may lower the value of its shares. Any prospective purchasers of the shares could use the tenant company's indemnity obligations as a bargaining chip and argue the price of a share should be reduced to reflect the risks inherent in such indemnities.

Maintaining business flexibility

Maintaining business flexibility to adapt to growth and source funding, address risks and respond to commercial needs is the cornerstone of a good business plan. Bricks and mortar obligations, however, are inherently inflexible, as are commercial leases.

Commercial leases drafted by or for a landlord provide the landlord with as much certainty – and as little risk – as possible. Of course, I can appreciate that, because the commercial leases I draft for my tenant medical practices sacrifice the interests of the landlord to ensure the flexibility of the tenant company. What you should be able to identify, as a potential lessee and tenant, are those clauses that protect the landlord *and* prevent or severely restrict your business flexibility.

As you or your lawyer negotiate a commercial lease, you should pay particular attention to the following clauses, which can reduce or disable your business flexibility:

- *Encumbering the lease:* Landlords' standard leases often prohibit the tenant from taking out a loan on the tenant's interest under the lease. Where the lease contains such a prohibition, and the tenant has taken out a loan on the tenant's interest under the lease, the tenant may find themselves in immediate default under the lease.

- *Subletting and assignment:* Although you may not foresee the need to sublet or assign the lease at the time you execute the lease, business circumstances often change. I have had clients who are tenants that have had restrictive subletting and assignment clauses which have enabled the landlord to benefit in return for allowing them the opportunity to achieve their revised business objectives.

Services

In a commercial lease, landlords will generally commit to ensuring that services (such as lifts, air conditioning and electricity) are available and in working order. It is advisable in reviewing the lease that a tenant request the lease include a rent abatement provision in the situation where important services are inoperative for any extended period. For example, if you have a patient with a disability who cannot access your practice for a month while the lift is not working, because they are unable to take the stairs, there could be damage done to your business beyond just the risk to the health of that one patient. If the clause is omitted, you may be obligated to pay the full amount of rent even though you're receiving customer complaints, suffering business losses or otherwise being negatively impacted by the unavailability of the service. Demanding inclusion of a rent abatement clause will also motivate the landlord to respond to service issues and repair requests as quickly as possible.

Other opportunities and issues

In addition to avoiding unnecessary risks and maintaining business flexibility, you should also consider the following issues when negotiating a lease:

- *Taxes:* You may be able to structure the fit-out of your property so that the expenses are depreciable, rather than being treated as capital works under the relevant taxation legislation. Structuring your business and fit-out properly has significant advantages, so it's worth getting tax advice before making the investment.

- *Payments to avoid make-good obligations:* Some landlords are willing to grant tenants an option to pay a pre-determined make-good amount in lieu of performing the required works and maintenance at the end of the tenancy. While any pre-determined amount should be carefully considered, it does provide you with the flexibility to continue business operations on the premises right up to the end of the lease term. Another option could be to vacate early, and continue to pay rent while the relevant make-good work is being performed.

- *Avoiding directors' guarantees:* If you want to assign your lease, the landlord will likely require you (or your company directors) to provide an ongoing guarantee of the lease. That is, you will be liable for any breach of an incoming tenant – even if you have no relationship to the tenant. Whenever possible, you should object to providing personal or directors' guarantees. The good news is that many landlords will accept a bank guarantee or security deposit instead. Securities are generally preferable because they are finite and easier to substitute.

- *Zoning/permitted use issues:* Leases invariably provide that the tenant is responsible for ensuring the 'permitted use' of the premises contemplated by the lease is compatible with the use permitted under local council planning and zoning laws. You may also be responsible for ascertaining and obtaining any approvals or licences necessary to operate your practice from the property. If you fail to obtain approvals or licences to do business and later discover your business cannot be legally conducted on the premises, you may still be obligated to pay the rent due under the lease. Depending on the circumstances, if your landlord was aware of the illegality of the intended use, he or she may be liable for your damages under a misleading or deceptive conduct claim. An opportunity to pursue a claim against your landlord may be of little solace, however, when you must disrupt your business to search for and secure a new location to resume operations.

Remember – the subjects covered in the preceding sections are a small sampling of many issues that may be relevant to negotiating the terms of your lease. Before negotiating the terms of a lease, you should brainstorm the potential issues that could negatively affect your business operations with your lawyer and accountant. When you are negotiating a new commercial lease, you need to take your time, consider your business plan and obtain advice as needed. In addition to avoiding substantial risks and costs, you will likely obtain greater insight, advantages and opportunities by consulting with expert negotiators and counsel who specialise in representing the best interests of private practice physicians.

LICENCE OR LEASE: UNDERSTANDING THE DIFFERENCE

If you operate your practice from within another leased business, you may be a sub-tenant or have a 'licence to occupy'. You may even be considering granting the right to use your leased property to another practitioner.

In any event, being aware of the difference between a lease and a licence is a good idea, because different legal rights are attached to each arrangement.

The fundamental difference between a lease and a licence is exclusive possession. I expand on this in the following sections.

Tenant under a lease

The earlier sections in this chapter covered leasing the property for your medical business, making you the property tenant. If you are a tenant under a lease, you have a legal interest, or 'proprietary rights' in the land.

Proprietary rights offer you the greatest protection under the law. As a tenant, you have a legal right to occupy the property and enforce that right against any third party. You also are afforded the protections of the Property Law Act and, where applicable, the Retail Leasing Act. These protections make it very difficult for landlords to unfairly or illegally terminate a lease.

Licensee

A licence, on the other hand, simply gives permission to enter and use the property for some stipulated purpose. The legal protections granted to tenants do not extend to licensees.

The rights of the holder of a licence (that is, the licensee) are based in contract, not property. A licensee:

- cannot enforce rights against third parties
- may or may not have exclusive possession

- may have a licence revoked by the party that granted it at any time
- termination of a licence may terminate any authority to enter the property (depending on the terms of the contract or agreement).

The terms 'lease' and 'licence' are sometimes used interchangeably. What is important to note is that even though your document may be identified as a 'lease' or a 'licence', a court asked to determine the rights held by a party is not limited by the title of the document and may examine the nature of the parties' relationship. The court will consider the parties' intentions and conduct prior to entering into the agreement, as well as the actual substance of the agreement.

Hopefully your primary takeaway from this chapter will be an increased understanding of the different financial arrangements and possessory interests in bricks and mortar. You may believe you are entering into a lease agreement when, in fact, you have only been granted a licence. Or you may intend to grant a licence to another business but end up conferring proprietary rights. You should be able to identify and explain the type of interest you intend to take or grant (whether lease or licence) before committing to an arrangement.

Granting a licence

If you are an existing tenant and want to grant a sub-lease or licence that extends to all or part of your leased premises, you will almost certainly need the consent of your landlord to grant this interest to a third party. You must first review the terms of the primary lease, and I also recommend you hire a lawyer to draft your sublease. In scenarios where a practitioner does *not* consult legal counsel before granting a sub-lease or licence, more often than not, the practitioner does not properly transfer their obligations under the primary lease to the sub-lessee or licensee and, therefore, the practitioner is forced to absorb the costs and responsibilities intended for the licensee.

PURCHASING PROPERTY

Very few medical practitioners or retailers purchase land or property from which to operate their practice. The obvious deterrents to purchasing property are the initial investment cost, the inherent risk of running a business, and the lack of flexibility.

If you are operating a stable and profitable private practice and are considering investing in property, you should first consult with a financial planner to iron out the tax and accounting implications. You should also ensure you have the most effective business structure (refer to chapter 9) in place to minimise your costs and risks.

13 ESSENTIAL ELEMENTS OF AN EMPLOYEE CONTRACT

Coming together is a beginning. Keeping together is progress. Working together is success.

Henry Ford (Founder of the Ford Motor Company)

An employment contract, whether written, oral or implied, consists of the terms and conditions governing the work relationship between an employee and employer. Generally, an employee agrees to provide certain services to an employer, who in turn promises to compensate (primarily via the payment of wages) the employee for those services.

For an employment contract to 'bind' or obligate the parties to carry out the terms of their agreement, the following contract elements must exist:

- offer and acceptance – the employer must offer the work arrangement to the employee, who must accept the terms of the offer
- both parties must intend to perform and abide by the terms of the work relationship
- 'consideration' must be given by each party to the other in exchange for the promises.

Consideration is something of value – a right, interest or benefit – each party will receive in exchange for the promises performed by the other party.

COMMON LAW CONTRACTS

Employment contracts arise from two primary sources of law: common law and statutory law. All Australian employees have common law contracts of employment, the terms of which have been established over time by the courts that decide employment disputes. In the absence of a written contract, common law employment terms will be implied in an employment agreement. These implied terms attempt to protect the rights of both parties balanced against the needs of the business.

A sound employment contract should anticipate conflict and include provisions to resolve potential disputes between an employer and employee. When the agreement is silent on an issue or the contract language is ambiguous or otherwise difficult to interpret, the courts will be called upon to interpret the terms. To prevent future disputes in the employment arrangement, what terms should your contract, at the very least, address? The following sections outline the areas to focus on.

Minimum legislative terms and industrial awards

Statutory employment terms are created by federal and/or state legislatures and appear in either workplace agreements (also known as 'enterprise agreements') or industrial awards.

Industrial awards are terms and conditions set forth in a legal instrument created by the Fair Work Commission or an industrial tribunal. These legislative terms and awards are designed to protect employees and ensure that everyone is paid at least the minimum wage.

Other sources, such as industrial instruments, workplace health and safety legislation and discrimination legislation will also apply to employment relationships. Any employment contract that does not comply or attempts to circumvent legislation will be rendered void and possibly give rise to criminal and personal penalties.

Workplace/enterprise agreements

Workplace or enterprise agreements set forth the reciprocal rights and responsibilities owed by the parties in one business or a group of businesses. These agreements allow employers to set employment conditions tailored to their business. The conditions in the agreements supplement – but do not conflict with – the minimum conditions in the National Employment Standards (NES). When a business has a workplace agreement, the industrial award does not apply.

Remuneration

One of the first – and generally considered the most important – terms of an employment contract is wages.

Your employment contract should not only include basic wages, however, but should clearly define whether wages include bonuses, commission, overtime hours, penalty hours and/or any other payment made such as incentives and employee expenses. The contract should also clearly state any relevant percentages and how calculations are made.

A straightforward annual or hourly wage contract may be simple enough to draft, but if your employment contract contains performance-based payments, commissions or other complex formulas, getting some expert advice may be wise.

Role responsibilities

Your employment contract should define the role of each employee clearly, including where and when the work is to be performed. If the role demands required outcomes, the stated results should be specifically defined and measurable.

Termination

Termination of employment is the most controversial aspect of employment law. Where an employment relationship has broken down and the contract fails to appropriately and clearly address termination, long, drawn-out conflicts can result – from which no real winners emerge.

Termination of employment can occur in several ways, including by:

- mutual agreement
- operation of time
- breach of agreement.

Termination by mutual agreement usually occurs when an employee tenders a resignation and this is accepted by an employer, or where the employer offers a redundancy accepted by the employee.

Notice periods for termination by agreement should be clearly stated in the contract, and they must also be reasonable. What is 'reasonable' will depend on the nature of the role, the seniority of the employee, length of service, and a host of other relevant factors. If you are unsure on what may be reasonable under the circumstances, you should consider consulting an attorney.

Termination by operation of time is used for projects or time-based contracts. The contract should clearly state both the length of the contract (for example, 12 months) as well as the termination date (for example, 31 December 2018).

Termination for breach of agreement can occur due to consistent or repeated failures to perform or exercise reasonable care and skill, or where a party to the contract has acted in a manner repugnant to the relationship. Termination for breach of contract in an employment setting is subject to additional legislative requirements and should be managed very carefully – again, consulting with an attorney is best.

Implied clauses

In the absence of anything to the contrary written in an employment contract, some terms may be implied purely due to the nature of the relationship, such as the employee's duty to exercise reasonable care and skill in the fulfilment of their role.

Confidentiality and protection of trade secrets are good examples of implied terms. It is, however, prudent to include them in an employment contract for certainty and clarity.

The following chapter looks at the practical aspects of employing people as you build your team.

14 BUILDING A TEAM

> My model for business is The Beatles. They were four guys who kept each other's kind of negative tendencies in check. They balanced each other, and the total was greater than the sum of the parts. That's how I see business: great things in business are never done by one person. They're done by a team of people.

Steve Jobs

My medical practitioner clients identify employee relations – which includes the hiring, managing and firing of employees – as one of the most difficult aspects of operating a business. Numerous federal and state laws apply to the employer–employee relationship, and an employer can be held liable for their conduct before a potential employee even interviews for a position (for example, via laws prohibiting discrimination in job advertisements). Similarly, employees can assert or enforce rights arising from employment long after the employer–employee relationship terminates (for example, via wrongful termination and wage claims).

In this chapter, I take you through some of these legal considerations, within the medical practice context as you continue to grow your business.

HIRING CHECKLIST

Ascertaining and complying with employer obligations can be both overwhelming and time-consuming. To help you with the task, I have provided a series of questions to use as a checklist before hiring a new employee.

Does your business structure allow you to take on an employee?

All business structures contemplate the need for staff, and all structures can employ them. Whether you're starting, running or growing your practice – and whether this is as a sole trader, partnership, corporation or trust – you can (cash-flow permitting) hire any number of employees.

What kind of employment are you offering?

Before you begin recruiting, you should consider how urgent the need to hire is, what tasks will be included in the job description, and how long you'll need to employ someone to finish the required work.

Before announcing the job opening, you should also determine the type of employees you will consider hiring for the position, including:

- permanent employees, whether full-time or part-time
- casual employees
- trainees or apprentices
- contractors (chapter 16 provides important information about hiring doctors as independent contractors)
- temporary employees through an employment agency or labour hire firm.

Employing people with different work arrangements can increase workplace flexibility and reduce overheads to more efficiently meet your practice's needs – just make sure you consider the full costs of each option.

Can your prospective employee legally work in Australia?

As an employer, it's your responsibility to make sure your employees can legally work in Australia. The analysis extends to employees sourced from a contractor or labour hire company and applies to both paid and unpaid work.

Employers may be liable for penalties assessed in connection with the hiring of illegal workers, even if they were unaware the individual was prohibited from working in Australia.

You also need to be aware that simply providing a tax file number (TFN) is not proof that an individual is authorised to work in Australia. Who can legally work is as follows:

• Australian citizens, Australian permanent residents, and New Zealand citizens are legally allowed to work in Australia.

• Australian visa holders are also legal workers if their visas specify authorisation to work. Some visas only allow the holder the legal right to undertake certain kinds of work. The authorisation may restrict the visa holder to working only for a specified employer, for example, for a maximum number of hours, or for a designated time.

Who cannot legally work is as follows:

• Some visas specifically prohibit the visa holder from undertaking any type of work.

• Foreign nationals without valid work visas cannot legally work in Australia. An invalid visa includes an expired or cancelled visa.

To verify whether a foreign national can legally work in Australia, employers can register with the Department of Immigration and Border Protection's free Visa Entitlement Verification Online (VEVO) system. In addition, a foreign national can verify work authorisation by emailing you his or her current visa details directly from the VEVO website or the myVEVO app.

What should you know about anti-discrimination laws?

All Australian workers have basic rights and protections in the workplace – such as the right to minimum pay and specified employment conditions. Employers can also be held legally responsible for acts of discrimination or sexual harassment that occur in the workplace or in connection with a person's employment. Federal and select state anti-discrimination and sexual harassment laws provide remedies to employees who have been unfairly or illegally refused or dismissed from a job; refused a promotion, transfer or other benefit associated with employment; given unfair terms or conditions of employment; refused training opportunities or flexible work arrangements; or harassed or bullied.

These acts can become unfair or illegal when the employee believes the discrimination or harassment has occurred due to the employee's:

- sex (this includes pregnancy, marital status or relationship – including same-sex and/or de facto – status, breastfeeding, family responsibilities, sexual harassment, gender identity, intersex status and sexual orientation)

- disability (this includes intellectual, sensory and psychiatric disabilities, diseases or illnesses; medical conditions; work related injuries; past, present and future disabilities; and association with a person with a disability)

- race (this includes colour, descent, national or ethnic origin and immigrant status)

- age (this includes younger and older people)

- sexual preference

- religion

- criminal record

- trade union activity

- political opinion.

Additional information on anti-discrimination and sexual harassment laws is available via the websites for the Australian Human Rights Commission (www.humanrights.gov.au) and Fair Work Ombudsman (www.fairwork.gov.au).

Remember that anti-discrimination and sexual harassment laws apply to not only employees but also contractors, part-time, full-time, casual or permanent workers, labour hire workers, workers on probation, commission or visas, and apprentices and trainees.

What are your record-keeping requirements?

As health care professionals, you are likely well-versed in the ethical, professional, and legal duties to safeguard patients' right to privacy and confidentiality regarding their medical records and health information. Although employment records are not as sensitive as patient records, employers owe a similar duty to comply with record-keeping requirements. Penalties may apply when an employer fails to meet business record-keeping and pay slip obligations. Business records must be retained for a much longer time than employment-related records.

A table outlining your record-keeping requirements in all areas of your business, including employment, can be found in appendix C. This can be used as a quick and easy reference guide to all record-keeping requirements.

Are you paying the correct wages and entitlements?

Australia's national minimum wage and ten employment standards, known as the National Employment Standards (NES), constitute the minimum entitlements guaranteed to most Australian employees. Sole traders operating in Western Australia (WA) and partnerships in WA's industrial relations system should refer to pay rates and hours of work, overtime and penalty rates specified for this state, because the NES and national minimum wages may not apply to you.

The minimum NES conditions

An employee's minimum wages, including penalty rates and overtime, are determined by the award or registered agreement that covers his or her employment (refer to the preceding chapter for more on employee contracts and agreements). An award will automatically apply to an employee if:

- it covers the business industry and type of work performed by the employee; and

- a registered agreement does not cover the business industry.

An employer cannot use or include any conditions in an employment contract, enterprise agreement or other registered agreement that:

- provide a pay rate that is lower than the rate in the relevant award
- provide a pay rate lower than the national minimum wage or the NES
- exclude the NES altogether.

Penalties may be assessed against an employer whose conditions fail to adhere to the NES in any way.

How to determine the appropriate award and pay rates

The various employment positions within the medical practice will attract different awards and pay rates. To help you work out which award and rate to apply to specific employees, the Fair Work Ombudsman has a Pay and Conditions Tool (PACT) that calculates your employees' pay rates, shift work and leave entitlements based on awards. You can also use PACT to find the correct award. (Go to calculate.fairwork.gov.au to find out more.)

Registering for the Fair Work Ombudsman's 'My Account' service allows you to save your PACT award results, and you will receive award updates by subscribing to receive email alerts.

What tax do you need to deduct from your employee's pay?

Under the Pay As You Go (PAYG) withholding rules, employers must collect tax from employee payments to ensure employees can meet their end-of-year tax liabilities.

Tax should be withheld if any of the following are true:

- you have employees
- you have other workers, such as contractors, and you have entered into voluntary agreements to withhold amounts from your payments to them
- you make payments to businesses that don't quote their Australian Business Number (ABN).

Penalties may apply if you don't comply with your withholding or reporting obligations. The ATO has a calculator tool on its website that can help you determine how much tax to withhold from your employees (go to www.ato.gov.au/calculators-and-tools/tax-withheld-calculator).

Electronic record-keeping and accounting packages (such as Xero, Quickbooks and MYOB) are also available that automatically calculate the amount of the tax withholdings.

What are your superannuation obligations?

Superannuation or 'super funds' are monies an employer pays its workers as a contribution to their retirement.

Employers must:

- Offer eligible employees a choice of super funds. Temporary residents are not eligible for a choice of funds.

- Pay the minimum amount, known as the 'superannuation guarantee' (SG). At the time of writing, this guarantee is 9.5 per cent of ordinary time earnings.

- Pay super contributions by each of the following dates: 28 July, 28 October, 28 January and 28 April.

If an employer fails to timely pay the SG to its employees' superannuation funds, the employer will be assessed and must pay an SG charge, which is not tax-deductible. In WA, sole traders and those operating under partnerships in the WA industrial relations system should refer to online information regarding the 'choice of super' (see www.commerce.wa.gov. au/labour-relations/choice-superannuation-fund-state-system).

Which employees are eligible to receive super?

In general, workers are eligible to receive super funds if they earn $450 or more (before taxes) in a calendar month.

Employers pay super funds to all eligible employees, including employees who:

- work on a full-time, part-time or casual work arrangement

- receive a super pension or annuity while still working, including those who qualify for the transition-to-retirement measure
- are temporary resident workers (at the time the temporary resident departs Australia, he or she may claim a 'departing Australia superannuation payment')
- act as a company director
- are a family member working for a family business, provided the worker is otherwise eligible to receive super funds
- are over 70 years of age.

Employers may also have to pay super for some contractors, even if the contractors quote an ABN (see chapter 16 for more on this).

What are employers' workplace health and safety obligations?

As a business owner, you are responsible for health and safety in your workplace. Under workplace health and safety laws, you must provide:

- safe premises
- safe machinery and materials
- safe systems of work
- information, instruction, training and supervision
- suitable working environments and facilities.

Procedures for maintaining a safe and healthy workplace should be implemented as part of your everyday business operations. Talk to your workers about potential health and safety issues, because they are in the best position to observe and report on any dangerous conditions that exist or arise on business premises or from operations.

Do you need workers compensation insurance?

As an employer, you must have insurance to cover workers if they are injured at work or become ill due to their work. This is known as workers compensation insurance. Workers compensation is covered by legislation in each state and territory. It's important to note that you may also need to cover contractors in certain circumstances. If you have any doubt, contact your lawyer or insurance broker.

Now we have the basics of employing people laid out, the following chapter looks at how to know the time is right to build your team.

15 GROWING YOUR TEAM

You can do anything but not everything.

David Allen (Author)

To paraphrase Shakespeare: 'To grow or not to grow, that is the question'. This book encourages self-reflection so you can focus on your zone of genius, examine the nuts and bolts of your business structure, and determine whether your business is prepared for growth. When you commit to expand, considering alternative business models, methods and theories will inspire you to realign your personal goals with your business vision. Along the way, I hope you will open up many new doors of opportunity and obtain greater access to your true potential.

From the get-go, making the decision to open a private practice was a huge step out of your comfort zone. Unless you're an entrepreneur by trade, launching a business can be pretty nerve-wracking. One thing I've learned from representing medical professionals is that many doctors struggle with the decision to hire the next employee or contractor, which is one of the first steps in expanding a business. Growth is a huge commitment, and when you increase your own responsibilities, you risk being overwhelmed. In this chapter, I take you through how to know when a new hire is needed, and how to understand the costs involved with *not* hiring new staff and expanding.

KNOWING WHEN THE TIME IS RIGHT

The choice to develop your business certainly should not be a haphazard one. The following sections outline some aspects to consider that may help you decide, or decline, to grow out your team.

Understanding practice trends and projections

Understanding your practice trends and projections is so important. Before you can decide if you're ready to hire a team member, you must first know whether your practice is growing, declining or holding steady. If your practice is growing, or even if it's stable, you should consider the positive impacts of hiring a team. However, if your practice is losing money or patients, you don't want to increase your financial responsibilities until your business is developing in a positive direction.

Identifying your current and ideal workloads

To help you work out your ideal workload, let's look at an example. Before Dr Kiddo opened up her paediatrics practice, she was working a demanding schedule at the Royal Children's Hospital, which included two night shifts a week at the associated clinic. Part of what motivated her transition to private practice was the desire to spend more one-on-one time with her patients and so deliver more personalised care to the community where she had lived her whole life.

After the first year in private practice, Dr Kiddo was ready to return to the hospital. Her patient load was manageable, but she was working longer hours than ever before handling the additional, unfamiliar tasks of running a business. After hiring an office manager and a bookkeeper, however, Dr Kiddo's practice began to run like a well-oiled machine. She earned a reputation for remembering important details about her patients' lives, which facilitated quick and accurate diagnoses and allowed her more time to explore treatment alternatives. Dr Kiddo received so many new patient referrals she was booked solid from 7 am to 7 pm six days a week. Dr Kiddo's increased appointments and lack of downtime now created another issue – she was back to facing as much stress and anxiety as she had faced in her first year of private practice.

When you started your practice, you probably found yourself working more hours than you'd ever worked as someone else's employee. In the beginning, you probably knew very little about operating a business and, like many new business owners, may have tried to save money by personally micromanaging every detail of the business. You can spend a lot of time researching and analysing various business methods, corporate compliance, accounting practices, landlord–tenant law, tax requirements, and myriad other issues relevant to operating a medical practice. This 'trial and error' method can be exhausting and means, when you make mistakes, you spend a lot of time correcting your errors, which further depletes your resources and energy. Thanks to the learning curve, however, you will eventually acquire the skills and experience necessary to turn a profit from your practice. You will learn what tasks to delegate to your team members and spend less time poring over the ins and outs of your business operations. Perhaps this is about where you are with your practice.

So how do you know when the time is right for hiring a team or adding new team members? One method of determining whether you're ready to bring on team members is to review your workload. How do you spend the majority of your time? Where do you want to spend the majority of your time? Understanding what tasks monopolise your efforts, and the extent to which certain tasks prevent you from focusing your energy on treating patients, will help you determine if you are ready to delegate some of your responsibilities to a new team member.

Knowing your financial situation and commitment

A comprehensive, personal knowledge of operating cash (ebb and) flow is another factor that will help you determine whether you're ready to hire a new team member. If you don't have any expectations concerning the receipt of monthly payments from insurers and patients, and don't know the deadlines for paying vendors and operating expenses, you probably won't be able to assess whether your practice can afford to pay a part-time administrative assistant's salary. And if you don't know the average total accounts receivables the business takes in each month, you won't know if this month's total exceeded or fell below the average.

In other words, if you don't understand the details of the cash flowing in and out of your business account, I encourage you to educate yourself on the issue.

CONSIDERING THE COSTS OF NOT HIRING

Growing a team is one of the first steps in developing your business. Your practice will thrive when you hire exceptional team members who share your vision and contribute their unique skills and experience to the business's common purpose. Also think about this in the reverse. What personality traits (including your own) could potentially obstruct team work, stunt business growth, reduce confidence, or otherwise throw a proverbial wrench in the cogs of your team and practice?

Inaction is a major theme in Shakespeare's *Hamlet*, and the fatal flaw of the play's tragic hero of the same name (as my paraphrasing at the start of this chapter alluded to). To think about this another way, one of the laws of physics states that each action (or inaction) has an equal and opposite reaction. Progress, then, cannot occur when team members or leaders are indecisive. In business, inaction can be equated with stagnation, and a failure to act reflects poor leadership. Your team will not trust or respect you if you overthink a response or fail to take necessary action when an opportunity presents itself.

I've already mentioned some of the red flags that militate against hiring a team or adding new members – for example, if your practice lacks financial stability or has lost patients to a competitor, it's probably not a good time to take on new team members. A business may lack the funds necessary to pay the costs associated with hiring; similarly, without understanding the business's cash flow, taking on a new payroll obligation would be unwise.

When your business has a need and can afford to hire but you can't find the time to interview applicants, the costs of *not* hiring a team member are less obvious. You may be asking yourself, how can a business lose money when it merely delays filling an open position? After all, the company saved not only the costs of finding, screening and interviewing applicants, but also the incidental costs of employment, including workers compensation insurance, superannuation, payroll taxes and salary.

When your business has a job vacancy and your team has more work than it can handle, the costs of *not* hiring can be either profits your practice loses by failing to capitalise on the opportunity, or intangible costs involving the negative consequences of too much work and not enough employees. If your practice loses revenue because you failed to hire someone to do a specific job for pay, you're losing profits. Other potential intangible costs include the negative effects (low morale, reduced productivity and/or errors, patients picking up on the negative atmosphere) arising from excessive work distributed among too few team members. And if the delay in hiring another team member has created a situation whereby work is not being timely completed, you might receive more complaints from patients, lose patients, or suffer irreparable damage to your business reputation.

IS OUTSOURCING AN OPTION?

Now that you've considered the potential costs of *not* hiring (or failing to timely hire) a new team member, you should also consider whether outsourcing could help your practice grow. When you outsource certain tasks, you have more time to devote to work that generates true income for your practice. Remember that outsourcing preferences vary from person to person. Ask yourself what work should be outsourced and avoid listening to everyone else's opinion on what you need. Your practice needs are personal, and outsourcing projects or tasks must fit the needs of the practice.

MAKING A DECISION

Over this chapter and the previous one, we've covered a lot of ground discussing the decisions related to hiring and building your team. Team selection is a *big* decision. Some hiring considerations will require more time and effort than others. You've also been warned about the consequences of inaction (that is, the delay in filling a job vacancy). You should try to anticipate your hiring needs well in advance so you have sufficient time to consider your options and prepare for selecting a team. Doing so will enable you to make smarter decisions before you burn out and hire the first candidate who walks into your office. Planning ahead and being proactive will help you determine the direction of your practice, what kind of team you need in order to reach your goals, and what your financial responsibilities will be.

During the hiring process, you can start mentally preparing to transition from the business owner mindset discussed earlier in the book to a specific subcategory of this mindset: the leadership mindset. Adapting to a leadership mindset requires a conscious shift in perspective, but I'm confident your medical career has prepared you for your new role as the effective leader of your private practice team.

16 MYTH BUSTING: CONTRACTOR DOCTORS

> When you do the right things in the right way, you have nothing to lose because you have nothing to fear.
>
> *Zig Ziglar (American Author)*

A business owner may be tempted to designate their workers as contractors because the cost of hiring an employee is greater than the cost of hiring a contractor. In addition to payroll tax requirements, hiring an employee requires the business owner to contribute to employee benefit funds such as workers and unemployment compensation.

However, by law, business owners are required to determine whether the workers they hire are actually employees or contractors – and, if they incorrectly classify workers as contractors instead of employees, they may be liable for penalties, interests and other charges. The adage 'It's just the way we do things around here' is a dangerous statement to make in any business, let alone a medical practice. And it will be no excuse if your practice is audited. This means the issue of worker misclassification is an important one to consider in the context of operating a private medical practice.

CLASSIFYING CONTRACTORS

The Australian Taxation Office (ATO) provides the following statement to explain the difference between an employee and a contractor:

'An employee works in your business and is part of your business. A contractor is running their own business.'

The ATO also identifies six common factors used to describe different characteristics of a work arrangement or relationship that indicate either an employee or a contractor classification. The indicators are as follows:

1   *Ability to subcontract/delegate:* This relates to whether or not the worker can pay someone else to complete the work (an employee can't whereas a contractor can).

2   *Basis of payment:* As an employee, payment is based on time worked, per item or activity provided, or commission. For a contractor, payment is based on a quote provided.

3   *Equipment, tools and other assets:* This relates to whether the business provides these (for an employee) or the worker does (as a contractor).

4   *Commercial risks:* An employee takes no commercial risks whereas a contractor does.

5   *Control over the work:* If the worker is your employee, you can direct how the work is performed, whereas a contractor can choose how they perform the required work.

6   *Independence:* An employee is not working independently from your business whereas a contractor is.

This means the first step in determining the proper classification involves comparing the facts of your actual work arrangements to the descriptions relating to either an 'employee' or 'contractor' in the preceding list. However, determining whether a worker is an employee or a contractor often involves analysis of additional factors to the ones listed. Further, no single factor will determine whether a worker should be classified as an employee or contractor, and the classification should be based on the totality of the relationship between the business owner and worker. All this means determining which factors to apply, and how much weight to give each indicator, can be difficult, depending on the specific facts of the work arrangement. To make things a little easier, the ATO provides further information in this area on its website, including an 'Employee or contractor decision tool' – just go to www.ato.gov.au/business/ employee-or-contractor.

You will also be less likely to misclassify an individual who works for your practice if you are aware of some widely held, but false, beliefs (otherwise known as 'myths') about the factors relevant to classifying employees or contractors. I cover these in the following section.

BUSTING COMMON MYTHS

Here I outline seven of the most common myths that cause private practice owners to misclassify a doctor's status as an employee or contractor.

A doctor who has an ABN is a contractor

A doctor is *not* deemed a contractor simply because he or she has an ABN. A doctor with an ABN may be properly classified as a contractor under one work arrangement, and properly classified as an employee under a different work arrangement. To determine whether the doctor is an employee or a contractor, you must look at all the facts ('the totality of the circumstances') of the work arrangement, as well as any specific terms and conditions applicable to the work being performed.

The relevant factors of the work relationship and/or arrangement should be analysed by an individual, preferably a lawyer, with current knowledge and expertise in worker classification laws.

Classifying doctors as contractors is standard industry practice, so all doctors are contractors

'Standard industry practice' is a legal term established by expert testimony in a court of law. Even if standard industry practice could be determined outside a court room, standard industry practice should not be equated with legal compliance. Furthermore, the law applicable to classifying workers is in a constant state of flux. The 'standard industry practice' for classifying doctors working in private practice may meet or exceed the corresponding legal requirements at a given time, but changes in the law could render the practice non-compliant at any time.

An alarming number of medical businesses do not consider the legal ramifications of their employment decisions, and many medical business owners regret their lack of foresight when the law catches up with them.

Doctors who work more than 80 per cent of their hours for one medical practice are employees of that practice

Some people think that if an individual works more than 80 per cent of the time for one company, the worker is classified as the company's employee. However, this 80 per cent Rule (also referred to as the 80/20 Rule) relates to personal services income (PSI) and determines whether an *individual* reporting contractor income on an individual tax return can claim some business deductions.

The 80/20 Rule is not relevant to a business owner's determination as to whether a doctor working for a private medical practice is an employee or contractor. The actual working arrangement needs to be examined, as well as the specific terms and conditions under which the work is performed, in order to properly classify a worker as either a contractor or an employee.

Business owners who classify doctors as contractors don't have to pay superannuation

Generally, contractors are not entitled to super, but an exception does exist. Contractors paid primarily for their labour are considered employees for superannuation guarantee purposes. A business owner must make super contributions for doctors classified as contractors if you pay them:

- under a contract that is primarily for the doctor's labour (more than half the dollar value of the contract is for labour)
- for personal labour and skills (physical labour, mental or artistic effort) and not to achieve a result
- to perform the contract work personally (delegation is not allowed).

If you hire doctors as contractors under the conditions stated in the preceding list, the practice would be required to pay the superannuation.

Doctors submitting invoices for payment are contractors

Submitting an invoice for services rendered or being 'paid on invoice' does not automatically make a doctor a contractor. At the risk of sounding like a broken record, to determine whether a doctor is an employee or contractor, you need to look at the entire working arrangement, as well as the specific terms and conditions under which the work is performed.

Doctors who ask to be contractors should be classified as contractors

A doctor's preference to work as a contractor is irrelevant to a proper classification. Whether a doctor is a contractor or employee is not a matter of choice. Even if both parties to an employment contract agree the doctor is a contractor, the agreement is not a determinant of the doctor's classification. Proper classification always involves a review of the entire working arrangement, as well as the specific terms and conditions under which the work is completed.

The practice has always classified doctors as contractors and never had any problems

As mentioned, employment law is subject to an ever-changing legislative intent. Federal and state legislatures are constantly revising, tweaking and changing the rules on how to classify contractors and employees. So even if your practice has always classified doctors as contractors, as a business owner, you are obligated to continue to consider the classification of the doctors you hire, and determine whether they are employees or contractors under the current law.

WHAT HAPPENS WHEN A NEW DOCTOR JOINS THE PRACTICE?

As already touched on in the previous section, you need to review the working arrangement for each doctor working in your practice to determine whether the doctor should be classified as an employee or a contractor. You need to perform this review whether the doctor is new to the practice or has been working for the practice for several years. If the first doctor you hired was classified as an employee, for example, that does not mean all the doctors you hire will be classified as employees.

I cannot stress enough that the determination must be made on the specific facts of the work arrangement.

WHAT TO DO NOW

There is no better time than the present to review your classifications. If you continue to classify doctors without reviewing the work arrangement, you may have a major problem to address. I've emphasised throughout this book that accepting the status quo is dangerous. Be rigorous when determining worker classifications and use experts to guide your decision-making. Regulators and others *are* watching. Keeping your hands clean now will save you money and time in the future.

17 MANAGING A PATIENT GRIEVANCE AND UNDERSTANDING COMPETITION LAW

Turn your wounds into wisdom.

Oprah Winfrey

Unfortunately, despite all your best endeavours, a time may come in your career when a patient has a grievance against your practice for the care you provided. An integral role of the Australian Health Practitioner Regulation Agency (AHPRA) is to protect the public and ensure continued high-quality health care. As part of this, AHPRA manages and deals with complaints (known as 'notifications') against registered health professionals.

Private health care practitioners are also subject to competition and consumer laws, enforceable by the Australian Competition and Consumer Commission (ACCC), and health businesses engaging in anti-competitive and unfair behaviour have been prosecuted in the past.

In this chapter, I take you through how to handle a patient grievance and notification to AHPRA, and what your obligations are under competition law.

WHAT TO DO WHEN AHPRA COMES KNOCKING

When an individual makes a notification to AHPRA, the agency works in coordination with Australia's National Practitioner Boards to investigate and resolve each particular case. Australia has 15 of these boards, covering a vast range of health services and specialties. The following sections outline how a notification might come about, how it then progresses, and what it might mean for your practice.

How might a notification be made against me?

Any person can submit a notification to AHPRA about a registered health professional. AHPRA is then responsible, in conjunction with the National Boards, for ensuring that relevant practitioners who are registered to practice have the skills and qualifications to provide safe care.

In certain situations health practitioners, employers or education providers are required by law to make notifications to AHPRA about a registered health professional. This includes situations where the practitioner is:

- practising while intoxicated
- engaging in sexual misconduct in connection with their practice
- practising while impaired
- practising in a way that is a significant departure from accepted professional standards.

How is the notification investigated and does this impact my ability to practise?

Generally, a notification submission, in and of itself, does not affect a doctor's ability to practise medicine. However, if the National Board determines a medical practitioner poses an immediate and severe threat to public safety, the doctor may be suspended from practice while the investigation is pending.

When a notification is lodged, the relevant National Board assesses the complaint and commences an investigation. This is a tedious process and can take up to 12 months. The person who lodged the notification will receive, upon completion, a response detailing the primary outcome of the investigation.

As you can imagine, every notification submitted to AHPRA is different, so even though a consistent procedure is in place for managing notifications, no standard response exists.

What should I do if a notification is made against me?

If you are a health professional and a notification has been made to AHPRA against your practice, the first thing you should do is call your professional indemnity insurance contact. You may face serious professional and legal implications, and your insurance contact will likely refer to you an experienced lawyer for assistance. And as with any investigative process, being proactive and on the 'front foot' through seeking advice early will work in your best interests and ensure you're well prepared.

Notifications made to AHPRA against a health professional's practice are taken very seriously. A response by the practitioner is required, and specific obligations may be included under your professional indemnity insurance. Even without professional indemnity insurance, a response must still be provided. A lawyer experienced in this area will be able to take you through what to include in your response and how to work with AHPRA through the review process.

How do AHPRA and the national boards work together?

Each of the national boards regulates their specific health profession, and all 15 are governed by the National Registration and Accreditation Scheme. The national boards and AHPRA work together to meet the objectives of the scheme.

A detailed list of the national boards and an explanation of how they work together can be found via the AHPRA website (www.ahpra. gov.au).

COMPETITION LAW FOR MEDICAL PRACTITIONERS

Like other retailers, private health care practitioners are private businesses, and as such are subject to competition and consumer laws. The federal legislation that addresses consumer law is the *Competition and Consumer*

Act 2010 (the 'Act') and the *Trade Practices Act 1974* (the 'TPA'). The ACCC is responsible for overseeing, investigating and enforcing the Act and the TPA. The ACCC has clearly indicated that the health sector is not immune to prosecution for anti-competitive and unfair behaviour, with several companies and health practitioners prosecuted for third line forcing and other anti-competitive activities.

The following sections look at how the consumer and competition laws apply to medical practitioners in these areas.

Third line forcing

Third line forcing (also known as 'exclusive dealing') occurs when a supplier forces a buyer or subscriber of services to exclusively use the services of another third-party supplier. Third line forcing is most commonly associated with franchises but can be seen across a range of industries and sectors, including health care. Examples include referrals to other service providers, such as radiology, pathology, and other specialists, such as anaesthetists.

Third line forcing will be in contravention of the Act where it has the effect of 'substantially lessening competition'.

Practitioners who operate in vertically integrated health care organis-ations – that is, where several primary services, such as a pathologist, chemist and general practitioner, are located under one roof – are most likely to be associated with allegations of third line forcing and need to be aware of these provisions.

To determine whether the behaviour has the effect of 'substantially lessening competition', consideration is given to whether refusal to supply a service restricts availability or whether patients are restricted in their ability to access a service.

Consider, for example, a general practitioner who agrees to provide health services to a patient provided the patient seek treatment from a specific specialist. Ostensibly, this does not, of its own, give rise to a breach. If, however, the general practitioner was the only GP in a small regional town, this arrangement could then be said to substantially reduce patient access to services. It would, therefore, fail the competition test, and the GP would be in breach of the Act.

Full line forcing

Full line forcing may occur when a GP and specialist, for example, agree that the specialist will prioritise the GP's patients before accepting any new referrals from another source.

Like third line forcing, full line forcing is in contravention of the Act where it has the effect of substantially lessening competition. However, the practice of medical referrals under the anti-competitive legislation remains a question of balance between protecting the community from unfair practices and providing the best, most efficient health care services.

One of the key issues for consideration by health practitioners when making referrals for other services will be informed patient consent. Make sure your patients are aware that they may choose a different specialist or see whatever imaging service or pathologist they wish.

Fee setting

Under the Act, doctors, like any other business owners, must set their consultation fees based on their practice structure only and may not engage in fee-setting behaviour with other practitioners.

Fee setting may occur when you agree with another practitioner not affiliated with your practice to:

- charge the same amount for consultations
- simultaneously increase or decrease fees
- collectively bulk bill certain patients
- collectively bulk bill all patients.

In most circumstances, this behaviour will be deemed price fixing and subject to penalties under the Act. However, some exceptions to the price fixing rule do exist for medical practitioners. A group of general practitioners who operate as a single practice may set a standard price. In these circumstances, patients are generally aware that they will be charged the same price regardless of which doctor they see. To be eligible for the exclusion from fee fixing, you must:

- ensure that your practice is structured appropriately
- seek approval from the ACCC to be excluded from the fee fixing provisions.

In circumstances where you do not practice either in partnership or through a shared legal entity, any agreement made with another practitioner regarding consultation fees will be fee fixing.

Misuse of market power

Section 46 of the Act prohibits an organisation that has significant market power from engaging in conduct that has the likely effect of reducing competition. Significantly, the test here is not whether the conduct did in fact lessen the competition but whether it was likely to.

While most Australian GPs remain small medical practitioners, we are beginning to see significant changes within the health industry. Medical centres are increasingly corporatised, and smaller practitioners have either merged into large conglomerates or incorporated into vertically integrated health practices. These practices, along with health insurers and private hospitals, are catching the attention of the ACCC.

Definitions of conduct that may contravene section 46 of the Act are broad and may include any action by an organisation that attempts misuse of their position. Misuse of market power may include some of the previously discussed behaviours, such as price fixing and third line forcing; however, a breach in this area can occur very easily from a range of other actions.

Examples of a misuse of position include using market power to:

- force another party to enter into a contract
- unfairly or unilaterally enforce a contractual provision
- employ unfair tactics to obtain a benefit
- act unconscionably to force another party to accept harsh or oppressive behaviour

- increase co-payments that result in increased prices
- bully or otherwise aggressively prevent new practitioners from entering the market
- attempt to limit the professional independence of health care professionals.

An example of unconscionable conduct in the health industry occurred recently when Medibank attempted to enforce a unilateral change to an existing contract with a small independent private hospital. The ACCC determined that Medibank was attempting to engage in unconscionable conduct via its size and position as Australia's largest health insurer, the degree to which the hospital relied on the contract that was in place, and Medibank's consistent refusal to discuss or negotiate the clause of the contract.

Medical rosters

Rural and regional areas of Australia rely heavily on medical rosters to ensure continual and sustainable health services can be provided to these communities.

In many cases, these medical rosters are run between doctors who practice through separate entities or hospitals, and would ordinarily be considered an anti-competitive arrangement in contravention of the Act. In a country as vast as Australia, however, shutting this arrangement down would have the unfortunate effect of cutting off essential medical services to rural communities.

The ACCC has established three requirements to ensure that medical rosters do not breach the Act:

1 *The purpose of the roster must be to facilitate access to medical services.* Providing access to medical services must be a key purpose of the roster, and this includes ensuring that doctors can maintain reasonable and sustainable working hours.

2 *Doctors on the roster must be able to practice even though they are not rostered on.* The roster must not prohibit or restrict when a doctor may practice. This does not mean that the roster cannot allow for

break times or minimum hours – only that the roster allows the doctor to work as many additional hours as they wish.

3   *Doctors on the roster must be able to see any patients they choose.* This means no restrictions can be placed on which patients a doctor may see. A roster that attempts to limit or inhibit a doctor from providing his or her services will breach the anti-competition provisions of the Act.

Consumer protection for patients

In addition to your professional obligations, you have the same obligations under the Act as a retailer or service provider to not mislead your patients or engage in unconscionable conduct.

You may not:

- mislead your patients as to your fees
- use misleading advertising
- mislead your patients as to your qualifications, experience or expertise
- mislead your patients as to procedures, treatment or outcomes
- act unconscionably or take advantage of patients who may require special care due to their education, infirmity, age, language, social, financial or other situational factor.

As always, if you have any questions or concerns in this area, speak with your lawyer.

PART V
THE BUSINESS MEDICAL

The health sector is currently facing significant reform – but when those reforms will happen, and what they will entail, remains to be seen. This uncertainty translates into stress for health practitioners. The fact is, the only thing a business owner can plan for is change. The previous parts have focused on ensuring your business is set for growth and profit. The chapters in this part focus on ensuring your practice has the strength and resilience to adapt and thrive in a changing environment through putting in place a strong practice model. Ensuring your business has quality service and programs, systems and processes within a flexible structure will provide your business the operational capacity and flexibility to adapt to a changing marketplace.

In the following chapters, I show you how to maintain this flexibility and stay ahead of the game, covering your marketing strategy and how to deal with technological disruption. I also cover preparing for your exit from the business at a time of your choosing – not when you're forced to leave.

18 MARKETING YOUR MEDICAL BUSINESS

Social Media is about the people! Not about your business. Provide for the people and the people will provide for you.

Matthew Goullart (Founder of Ignite Digital)

Warning: don't post anything on social media until you've read this chapter.

We all know social media is the new 'black' when it comes to marketing and advertising, with the ability to deliver real benefits to business revenue. As you continue to grow and scale your medical business, marketing on social media should be an important part of your overall marketing plan. But can doctors and medical professionals use social media? How should they use it? And what legal and ethical issues are at play here? In this chapter, I cover how the relevant legislation applies to medical business, and what approach you should be taking in your marketing.

UNDERSTANDING THE LEGISLATION

With several relevant pieces of legislation in place, navigating advertising standards for medical practices and health service providers can be a minefield, particularly when it comes to social media. The following sections take you through some of the common concerns, and how to handle them.

What exactly does the law say about advertising medical services?

To date, the Health Practitioner Regulation National Law (the 'National Law') does not contain a specific definition of 'advertising'; however, advertising has been interpreted as encompassing all forms of printed and electronic media, including social media.

Therefore, it is essential doctors understand the impact of providing medical information on social media platforms, including replying to a comment on Facebook, posting a link on Twitter or writing an article on LinkedIn. All these actions are considered 'advertising' under the legislation, even if the doctor's intention is simply to provide feedback, information or respond to a question.

Which laws actually apply?

Before we go on to navigate this tricky landscape further, considering the principles behind the National Law may be useful. Advertising guidelines in the medical industry are designed to protect consumers and patients from false and misleading information that may compromise their health care choices.

The law relating to medical advertising derives from several sources. The most important source is the already mentioned 'National Law', which governs advertising for health practices and services. Another source is the Therapeutic Goods Advertising Code 2007 (the 'Code'), which contains provisions relating to the advertising of medicine, vitamins and medical devices.

In addition to these industry-specific laws, the *Commonwealth Competition and Consumer Act 2010* and the Fair Trading legislation of each state and territory also apply. These impose standards for advertising and obligations to conduct your business in a manner that guarantees consumer safety and the provision of suitable products and services.

How do I know what are acceptable types of advertising?

Fundamentally, advertising of medical and health services must be factual, accurate and clear. For example, if your advertising creates unrealistic expectations as to the effectiveness of the medication or service you provide, you will fall foul of the National Law. This includes using sweeping statements such as 'achieve the look you want', or 'look better and feel confident'.

Similarly, if your practice promotes inappropriate or unnecessary use of health services, you will also be breaching the National Law. Examples of this kind of advertising include using phrases such as 'Don't delay' or 'Get your test results today'.

Any statement that misleads or, more importantly, may be likely to mislead a consumer contravenes the National Law. The distinction here is important because the legislation will not consider whether the statement did, in fact, mislead anyone – only that someone, particularly those who may be vulnerable, could be misled.

What does this mean for social media?

The informal nature of social media makes use of these platforms a particularly perilous affair for doctors. Casually commenting on a Facebook post about recovery times, for example, constitutes improper advertising, as does recommending a treatment or medicine without fully disclosing all associated risks.

Providers of plastic surgery, weight loss treatments, skin care and beauty treatments run the most risk of violating the advertising laws. You likely don't have to scroll too far through your Facebook feed to see claims like 'Get the flu shot before the flu gets you', or 'Bone density testing FREE today!' These statements, while they promote valuable and legitimate health services, could, as stand-alone statements, fail to meet the standards of the National Law, and prompt the regulator to come knocking.

The use of images, particularly the use of 'before and after' photos are also heavily regulated under the legislation. Images must depict a real patient who has fully consented to the use of his or her image for advertising purposes. If the picture represents a before and after image, the set up for each photo must be the same or substantially the same, including lighting, background, framing, exposure, posture and clothing.

What are the implications for non-compliance?

It's important to note that private practice owners cannot delegate their duties under the legislation. Practitioners must read and expressly authorise any and all content that promotes a health service or therapeutic product, including articles or media reports (advertorials). In other words, they can't deny responsibility because someone else actually wrote the content.

In addition to fines of up to $5,000 for an individual and $10,000 for a corporate entity, breach of the National Law advertising standards will trigger disciplinary action by professional bodies for unprofessional conduct. Consequences for a violation of professional conduct standards are broad but can include restriction on practice or, ultimately, revocation of your practicing certificate.

WITH ALL THIS IN MIND, SHOULD I EVEN BE USING SOCIAL MEDIA?

Yes, definitely. Social media is a legitimate communication channel, and one which doctors can benefit from using. It's important, however, to consider the professional ramifications of what you are posting, where you are posting it and what claims you are making.

19 THE FEAR OF DISRUPTION IS IRRATIONAL

> Anxiety, the next gumption trap, is sort of the opposite of ego. You're so sure you'll do everything wrong you're afraid to do anything at all. Often this, rather than 'laziness', is the real reason you find it hard to get started.
>
> Robert M Pirsig, Zen and the Art of Motorcycle Maintenance: An Inquiry into Values

One uncertainty that some medical professionals find particularly unsettling in the current environment of change is disruption. This is a word that sends shivers down the collective backs of business owners the world over, in every single industry and profession. Think about Uber, Airbnb and Netflix. These and companies like them have caused enormous change and disruption in their respective industries. As the world continues to change, disruption is a word we hear a lot these days. Technology has exploded and continues to severely upset and disrupt many industries, and the medical industry is no exception.

In this chapter, I offer some tips for dealing with disruption, and cover why it might not be such a bad thing, especially when it comes to HealthTech.

DEALING WITH DISRUPTION

I recently learned about a medical practice that bought a machine that, through the efficiencies it created, wiped out one-third of the old business. The practice owners knew that embracing robotic surgery had major benefits to patients because it allows minimally invasive, highly accurate laparoscopic procedures. It also significantly reduced hospital stays for their patients.

So, even though they knew the new technology would wipe out some of their business, the specialists also knew the machine was better for patient outcomes, so they considered the investment in the machine worthwhile, and then they managed its impact on the business.

When it comes to disruption, the big questions you should be asking are:

1 What exactly is disruption? (Tip – it's not what you think.)

2 Is it a threat or an opportunity?

What is disruption?

The term 'disruption' really took off 20 years ago with Clayton Christensen's 1997 book, *The Innovator's Dilemma*. Here, Christensen explained that disruption comes from not only meeting customers' current needs but also anticipating their unstated or future needs. Henry Ford reportedly said, 'If I had asked people what they wanted, they would have asked for a faster horse.' Although no evidence exists of Ford actually saying this, the general idea holds – Ford recognised that sometimes people do not know what they need.

Netflix is a perfect example of a disrupter of its own industry. Originally operating as a DVD mail order company, it was a valid business, but the leaders knew that mail order was not going to be sustainable in a technology driven environment – customers weren't always going to want to wait three days for the post to arrive. They worked quietly but relentlessly in the background, building their online streaming and on-demand business in an attempt to disrupt their own business model. They approached Blockbuster for a collaboration but were knocked back. When Netflix launched on-demand movies, Blockbuster went bust. Blockbuster had failed, quite dramatically, not only in recognising an opportunity, but also in anticipating their customers' future wants and needs.

Within the medical industry, the opportunities for disruption abound, especially in Australia where the health care system is somewhat fragmented. Despite our best efforts, it can sometimes feel like GPs exist in a silo, and systems for coordinating care between specialists aren't meeting the needs of patients. Costs are rising astronomically, while the government does not seem to recognise this. In addition, patients are increasingly frustrated with the disconnect between their holistic health needs and an industry unable to meet them.

We are already starting to see disruption in the way patients engage their GP – forgoing travel time and waiting rooms in favour of virtual doctor appointments. The Internet of Medical Things (IoMT) is changing the way medical devices collect and record information. Their applications are endless, but the most well-known and popular at a consumer level are wearables such as a Fitbit or Garmin product. Although perhaps seen as accessories for fitness junkies, wearables such as these provide us with just one of the technologies available for capturing clinical data that allow doctors to measure and diagnose a patient's physiological condition remotely.

Is disruption a threat or an opportunity?

Healing is a matter of time, but it is sometimes also a matter of opportunity.

Hippocrates

Disruption is an opportunity to increase efficiency and margins, simplify processes and increase services, through technology and collaboration.

Netflix was criticised when they set their goal to launch online on-demand movies. Naysayers told them they were going to disrupt their own business model – that is, mail order movies – and they did, of course. But this foresaw future needs – although Netflix in the US still sends out DVDs, very few people still order movies by mail and they don't offer this service in Australia. The key takeaway, however, is that Netflix was not afraid of disrupting their own business model because they recognised an opportunity.

You can embrace disruption in the medical industry in a variety of ways, but no 'one size fits all' solution is possible. Being aware of what disruption is and how it happens is the most important start. Getting to deeply understand your patients is the next step. Then you can consider day to day which parts of your practice may be vulnerable to disruption and start developing an innovation plan.

Invest in your innovation plan

Being able to innovate starts with developing strong relationships with your patients, and knowing what their future needs and wants are. Encourage your team to contribute ideas, connect with colleagues and keep abreast of the new technologies and possibilities.

Disruption is not demolition. It is an opportunity to embrace new possibilities for your practice and your patients.

CONSIDERING HEALTHTECH

After almost a whole chapter on disruption, not talking about some of the amazing innovations coming out in the HealthTech space would be a mistake. As you already know, in our modern world technology is a crucial ingredient of health care. All health care consists of either human interaction, the use and application of technology or a combination of both.

In Australia an explosion in the development of digital health care tools has occurred. I recently saw HealthTech described as 'the new black' of start-ups. There is a rise of chronic disease which increases the need for continuous connected care, and for many people time is of the essence. Having experienced medical practitioners involved in the development of HealthTech innovations is critical, and will likely transform how medicine is practised.

As HealthTech is really still only in its early stages, perhaps we are at the brink of significant technological breakthroughs – think about what artificial intelligence and machine learning will be able to facilitate. Also think about how you can stay abreast of these changes – and take advantages of them for the improved health of your patients and your business.

20 DETERMINING THE FINANCIAL VALUE AND COMPLIANCE REQUIREMENTS OF YOUR PRACTICE

Health is like money, we never have a true idea of its value until we lose it.

Josh Billings

As we approach the end of the book, it's time to talk about a possible end game for your practice. If you follow the steps I have laid out, by the time you're ready to leave the practice you will have created a valuable foundation. As an owner, your exit strategy will focus on 'practice valuation'.

Even if you have no present intention to leave your practice, you should spend some time planning for it because it could very well be one of the largest financial transactions in your lifetime. While you can make an excellent living operating your practice with a doctor's mindset, making decisions from a business owner and/or leader mindset will enable you to create and receive value for the practice you build.

Determining the value of a medical practice involves a variety of issues beyond the coverage of this book. As a quick summary, you should consider keeping metrics on referral patterns (to your practice from other doctors), along with the practice's insurances, the economic climate, and the practice specialty. These are all relevant to the valuation. You also need to consider what age you would like to be when you exit, because whether or not you are staying on with the practice for an extended period of time could be relevant to your buyer. The single largest driving factor in the value of a practice is the cash flow available for the buyer.

In this chapter, I cover how fair market value is determined, along with why setting up a compliance program for your business could make it more valuable.

DETERMINING FAIR MARKET VALUE

This might surprise you, but there can be two medical practices in the same geography, with the same specialty, that may have two different fair market valuations. 'How can this be?' I hear you throwing your arms in the air and crying out. This occurs due to additional criteria considered to establish the fair market value, which include:

- efficiencies
- operations
- profitability.

Do you think that selling a medical practice is a lot like selling any other business? You might think that, as with other business investments, a buyer will look for a return on their investment in the form of cash flow and the potential for growth.

Most experts agree, however, that both art and science contribute to the process of preparing a business valuation for a medical practice. That includes understanding the risks that will go into the valuation of the practice and the economic environment, which can help to determine the likely cash flow stream.

If you are a seller, you are likely to want the sale price to reflect your effort (some call this 'sweat equity', or the unpaid efforts arising from time invested) to build the practice, its reputation, and the revenue it will continue to provide to the new owner.

The valuation will take into account tangible and financial assets, patient accounts receivable, your practice's office building, goodwill and intangible assets. Tangible and financial assets include the practice's equipment and furniture, cash, prepaid insurance (unexpired insurance premiums), and other assets minus liabilities, including payroll taxes, loans and superannuation contributions.

A word about goodwill

Goodwill is the most subjective and variable asset. Valuing the intangible assets and goodwill of a medical practice can be a contentious issue, depending on who the buyer of the practice is.

If the practice or related entity owns the office building, and the office is leased, the leasehold may have a value depending upon the number of years remaining, amount paid for rent compared to going market rent, and the ability to renew the lease. Some buyers can see a lease as an asset, but some may see it as a liability.

Office location and profitability are also important – again, depending on who your buyer is. A buyer will be willing to pay more for a more profitable practice.

There are a number of factors that can affect the value of goodwill, which is often dependent upon the ability of the purchaser to be able to earn a higher return from the practice compared with what could usually be expected to be earned by the doctors in the specialties represented in the practice.

If you are thinking of selling your practice, make sure you consult with a broker who is an expert in selling medical practices within your specialty. As with any high-stakes negotiation that you are planning, consulting an expert is one of the most important steps in setting yourself up for success.

BUSINESS OBLIGATIONS AND COMPLIANCE

Medical practices are a highly regulated type of business (in contrast, for example, to a furniture removal business, which has hardly any regulation). Compliance is a term that is used to describe a business program designed to prevent and detect breaches of any laws, regulations, standards or codes with which businesses must comply. Many different laws and regulations govern the operation of Australian businesses, and many apply to the highly regulated health profession. Some compliance issues affect businesses generally, especially if the business is incorporated and running under a company structure. Some of these regulations are found in the *Corporations Act 2001* (Cth); there are also industry-specific regulations, and company policies can also apply and be enforceable on the business as well as the team members.

Why do medical practices have compliance programs? Consider the following:

1   *It makes good business sense.* A well-designed compliance program will give you greater visibility regarding the day-to-day activities within the business. Also, you may want to do business with companies that require a practice to have a corporate compliance program in place.

2   *Staff benefit from having standards and procedures to follow that make doing their jobs easier.* Team members can thrive knowing what is permitted and expected, and it also allows them to focus on the task at hand. Importantly for the owners of a practice, a compliance program also helps reduce the prospect of criminal conduct.

3   *Many industries, including health-related industries, have their own codes of conduct.* Having a compliance program in place makes it easier for a business to state it follows the code when the regulators come knocking.

4   *It makes it easier for a business to comply with legislative requirements.* A compliance program allows a business to ensure that all staff (in particular new staff members) know and understand the company's legal requirements. Whether these be workplace health and safety, privacy or ASIC requirements, a compliance program will ensure that your business is up to date on its collective legal requirements.

As you start to think about an exit plan for your business, having a compliance program in place can also make the business more attractive to potential buyers.

Is my practice too small to have a compliance program?

While it may feel like it, no, your practice is never too small to have a compliance program. It is sensible to tailor any program to the size and type of practice you run. Even if you are running your business as a contracting doctor (with no employees), having a compliance program will enable the proper documentation of essential business procedures, such as accounting. When I first started my business You Legal and I was running as a sole practitioner, I missed a tax payment. I had the money in the account but was distracted giving legal advice to clients, rather than keeping my eye on the compliance requirement. I received a fine from the ATO, and it was the financial hit that I needed to put my own compliance program in place.

Starting a well-designed compliance program early in your journey, like I did, can mean that, as your practice grows, employees will understand their obligations in the areas of privacy, intellectual property, and dealing with regulators and other staff, to mention just a few.

What should my compliance program cover?

If your practice is running as a company, a compliance program should, at a minimum, cover all of the company legal requirements. This is often something that your book-keeper, accountant or lawyer will assist with. You may already know this, or have delegated the responsibility to another person, but these include the following:

- A registered office in Australia. ASIC must be informed of the address, and you must update the records with ASIC when you move.

- If you run the business from a location that is different from the address of your registered office (which ASIC calls your Principal Place of Business), you must let ASIC know the address.

- ASIC must be informed of the names of the directors of the business and any company secretaries as well. ASIC must have an up-to-date list of the directors and company secretaries, including their full names (and any former names), date of birth and home address.

- A legal requirement exists to pay all relevant fees to ASIC. This is so important, because if you fail to do this, ASIC may de-register the business. This has happened to clients of mine, who have been particularly distressed at the possible implications, as you can imagine.

As you start to think about preparing your business for sale and ensuring the highest possible valuation, you can also think about your personal succession plan – the topic of the next chapter.

21 PERSONAL SUCCESSION PLANNING

Doing good to others is not a duty, it is a joy, for it increases our own health and happiness.

Zoroaster

Every day in your job, you deliver health news that people do not want to hear or accept. I have noticed that some of our doctor clients seem to have a mindset that they are immune to receiving bad health news themselves. While it's great to be optimistic, it is also important to be realistic. And regardless of when you are thinking about exiting your business, having your personal succession plan in place is always important.

In this chapter, I cover having a legal will in place and considering the impact of where your money goes.

ORGANISING YOUR WILL

Having a legal will is important. As I write this, I acknowledge I must take my own advice. Although I already have a legal will, it has not been updated since I started You Legal four years ago. Updating a legal will is just as important as establishing a legal will. Personally, the last thing I would want is a dispute over the assets of my estate.

Wills are highly technical documents

Some highly intelligent doctors have asked me whether it's okay to use a DIY 'will kit'. You could do this, but as with any area where we dabble and are not experts, unclear drafting or a technical deficiency in your will may cause disputes between family members or other beneficiaries of the will. This can result in estates being significantly reduced because legal fees incurred come from the estate rather than from those challenging the will.

A will can provide for other important considerations

A will also allows you to appoint guardians for your children, express your wishes regarding your funeral and burial, and provide for many other important considerations.

When having an original will prepared or updating your old will, think about the following:

- the possibility of losing the ability to make decisions for yourself through accident or illness
- appointing others to make financial decisions (Enduring Power of Attorney) on your behalf
- appointing others to make medical and lifestyle decisions (Advance Care Directive) on your behalf.

These are all documents you know all too well because you have lived and breathed them (or the lack of them) through your work. Regardless of the size of your estate, the number of assets you own, or whether you have children provided for under insurance policies or your superannuation fund, having a well-prepared will in place at the time of your death makes it much easier for your loved ones to manage your affairs during a time that will no doubt be very difficult for them.

CONSIDERING THE IMPACT OF GIVING

Even though it may not always feel like it, as professionals and business owners living in Australia we are luckier than most people on the planet.

This has come about through the luck of where we have been born, and through our grit and determination. As a lawyer, I have often felt an obligation to give back to those less fortunate, and with my skills that is usually those within my direct community or the wider community in Australia.

As a business owner, you do more than most to help the community because you employ people, and as a medical professional you are helping people day in day out through your work. I get that and I feel that way too but, lately, I have started asking people in my team what their big goal is, and what it is that they want out of life. It's been fascinating to hear what they have to say, to get to know them and what makes them tick more deeply, so I can be a better leader.

These conversations have led to a discussion within the firm about what matters to everyone as a whole. We already have strong values, as I discussed in the introduction, and all of our team members are a value match with the organisation, and so we have used these discussions as an opportunity to connect with each other.

In discussing what matters to us, we have also discussed our workplace giving program. While we do pro-bono work for clients who match our values, like many other firms, and our team members sit on boards where they believe they can make an impact, in the past we have struggled to find a cause that unites us. This meant our giving hadn't found a focus – we have donated to not-for-profits through the sale of my books, for the birthdays of members of our community, for people who have referred clients to us and so on. And we were left wondering, what could our team do that would make an impact in a directed way to help the planet.

It was then that I discovered that in September 2015 the United Nations General Assembly adopted the 2030 Agenda for Sustainable Development that includes 17 Sustainable Development Goals (SDGs) to transform our world. The principle that they are working towards is 'no-one left behind'. This agenda emphasises a holistic approach to achieving sustainable development for all.

The SDGs are:

- Goal 1: No Poverty
- Goal 2: Zero Hunger
- Goal 3: Good Health and Well-Being for people
- Goal 4: Quality Education
- Goal 5: Gender Equality
- Goal 6: Clean Water and Sanitation
- Goal 7: Affordable and Clean Energy
- Goal 8: Decent Work and Economic Growth
- Goal 9: Industry, Innovation and Infrastructure
- Goal 10: Reduced Inequalities
- Goal 11: Sustainable Cities and Communities
- Goal 12: Responsible Consumption and Production
- Goal 13: Climate Action
- Goal 14: Life Below Water
- Goal 15: Life on Land
- Goal 16: Peace, Justice and Strong Institutions
- Goal 17: Partnerships for the Goals

After finding out about these goals, the You Legal team reviewed them and considered which ones were most important to us as a team. Based on this, we undertook that the profits from each book sold by You Legal from that point on would provide a young person living in a remote indigenous community the chance to develop IT and English literacy skills by providing a safe space for one day, for enhanced learning and capacity building.

The SDGs that this giving relates to are:

- Goal 4 – Quality Education
- Goal 8 – Decent Work and Economic Growth
- Goal 9 – Industry, Innovation and Infrastructure
- Goal 10 – Reduced Inequalities

For more information on the UN's SDGs, go to http://www.un.org/ sustainabledevelopment/sustainable-development-goals. If you would like to find out more details on the giving impacts that You Legal has committed to, information is available on our website (www.youlegal. com.au).

In my view, one of the most important parts about giving is having a cause that resonates with you and your team.

CONCLUSION

> To keep the body in good health is a duty ... otherwise
> we shall not be able to keep our mind strong and clear.
>
> *Buddha*

My great hope is that you have come to the end of this book with an action plan for your practice. I also hope you are feeling less frustrated and overwhelmed than you were when you picked up the book.

As you know, medical schools teach the mechanics of being a great doctor, while hospital and specialist training help medical professionals find their niche. What they do not do is equip those who take care of our community when they are most vulnerable with the skills to effectively run a thriving business.

Throughout this book, we have looked at the issues that arise in running medical businesses – from why we need to put contracts into writing and reviewing your business structure, to employment law and using contractors, intellectual property and competition law and privacy compliance. I have also spent some time looking at modern leadership techniques and entrepreneurialism and given you a glimpse into the future with some ideas about how to examine your medical practice for the best possible outcomes by thinking about technology and innovation in your business.

Now you are ready to approach your business with a business and leadership mindset, and one that aligns with your goals. Good luck – and let me know how it goes.

APPENDIX A

SAMPLE OPERATIONS MANUAL: TABLE OF CONTENTS

Here I've provided a sample table of contents for an operations manual and a table outlining your record-keeping requirements in different areas. All medical businesses are different and you will need to create an operations manual that works for you and your staff. You can use the following sample table of contents to start thinking about the areas your operations manual needs to cover and how the content can be organised.

1 **Practice**
   - 1.1. Philosophy (Mission, Vision, Values)
   - 1.2. Identification (Name, Address, Phone, Website, Driving and Parking Directions, etc.)
   - 1.3. Tools for Patients
   - 1.4. Doctors' Biographic Summary
   - 1.5. Hospitals
   - 1.6. Outpatient Facilities
   - 1.7. Insurance Accepted
   - 1.8. Cash Pay Fee Schedule
2 **Clinic Maintenance by Clinic Staff**
3 **Incoming Communication**
   - 3.1. Telephone Calls
   - 3.2. Mail
   - 3.3. Faxes
   - 3.4. Email
   - 3.5. Text Messages

4   **Outgoing Communication**

- 4.1. Telephone Calls

- 4.2. Mail

- 4.3. Faxes

- 4.4. Email

- 4.5. Text Messages

- 4.6. Overnight or Messenger

5   **Out-of-Office Services**

- 5.1. Record

- 5.2. Rounds on In-Patients

6   **Clinic Schedule**

- 6.1. Guidelines

- 6.2. Organisation by Day and Clinic Session

- 6.3. Walk-Ins

- 6.4. Running Behind Schedule

- 6.5. Scheduling Guidelines

7   **Inpatient, Outpatient, and In-Office Procedures**

- 7.1. Plan

- 7.2. Guidelines

- 7.3. Cardiovascular clearance requirements

- 7.4. Process

8   **Charts**

- 8.1. Organisation

- 8.2. Guidelines

- 8.3. Preparation for visit

- 8.4. Location and Progression of Charts (Note: Paper Charts; EHRs have their own issues)

9   **Clinic Visit**
  - 9.1. Reception
  - 9.2. New Patients
  - 9.3. Rooming
  - 9.4. Exam
  - 9.5. Discharge
  - 9.6. Test Orders
  - 9.7. Labs

10 **Test Orders**
  - 10.1. Labs
  - 10.2. Requisitions
  - 10.3. Results

11 **General and Administrative**
  - 11.1. Clinic
  - 11.2. Contracts
  - 11.3. Insurance
  - 11.4. Security
  - 11.5. Professional
  - 11.6. Pharmaceutical/Medical Device Representatives
  - 11.7. Staff
  - 11.8. Inventory Management

12 **Procedures**
  - 12.1. Certified Mail
  - 12.2. Form Letters
  - 12.3. Prescriptions
  - 12.4. Refills and Changes

13 Forms

- 13.1. Form Letters
- 13.2. New Patient Triage
- 13.3. Patient ID Labels
- 13.4. Procedure Information Forms
- 13.5. Procedure Scheduling Form

14 Policies

- 14.1. Cyber Risk
- 14.2. Privacy Policy
- 14.3. Patient Payment Terms
- 14.4. Complaints Process
- 14.5. Quality Control Process
- 14.6. Consent and Patient Management Processes
- 14.7. Response to High Risk Patients (Infectious Diseases)
- 14.8. Workplace Health and Safety
- 14.9. Hazards
- 14.10. Ordering and Supply Chain Policy
- 14.11. Cold Chain Policy
- 14.12. Power Outage Policy
- 14.13. Breach Reporting Policy
- 14.14. Waste Disposal Policy (including sharps)
- 14.15. Adverse Events Reports
- 14.16. Recording and Reporting Process
- 14.17. Delegations
- 14.18. Confidentiality Policy
- 14.19. Contract Policy
- 14.20. Tender Management
- 14.21. Freedom of Information
- 14.22. Intellectual Property
- 14.23. Conflicts of Interest (Board members and staff)

APPENDIX B

SHAREHOLDERS' AGREEMENT CHECKLIST

1 **Establishment of Shareholders' Relationship:**
   - Who are the shareholders (including names of relevant companies, individuals or trusts who stand behind those entities)?
   - What are the number and class of shares held or to be subscribed for?
   - Are there any rights to attach to different classes of shares (for example, will there be different voting, capital, dividend, veto rights)?

2 **Board of Directors and Company Officers**
   - Who will be the Directors of the Company?
   - How will Directors or replacement Directors be nominated? For example, will each shareholder be entitled to appoint a Director?
   - How will Directors be removed and in what circumstances? Are Directors only to be removed by the shareholder appointing them or will they rotate?
   - How will Directors' fees and remuneration be determined (if any)?
   - What sort of insurance and other protection will Directors require?
   - Who will be the Company Officers initially and how will they be appointed afterwards?

- Will there be any limitations to powers and responsibilities for any Director(s)?

- Will Directors be able to appoint alternate Directors?

3 Directors' Meetings and Resolutions

- What will be the procedure for Directors' meetings, including:

  › quorum

  › voting entitlements; and

  › board decisions?

- Will unanimous approval, special approval or other majority be required for particular issues, such as borrowing from a third party, entering into a lease or purchasing or selling a significant asset? (These may be issues Directors resolve. Alternatively, some decisions may require shareholder approval.)

4 Shareholders' Meeting

- What will be the procedure for shareholders' meetings, including:

  › calling of meetings of shareholders

  › quorum

  › shareholders' resolutions?

For example, will unanimous approval, special approval or other majority be required for particular issues?

5 Dividend/Distribution Policy

- How will the Company's dividend distribution policy be determined:

  › at Directors' discretion;

  › at shareholders discretion; or

  › determined in advance (for example, 75% of profit in every year)?

6 Financing of the Company

- Will shareholder contributions be required? If so, how much? What about in the future? For example, if the Company requires additional finance for the operation or expansion of the Company, should shareholders be obliged to contribute additional equity in proportion to their shareholding? What happens if there is a shortfall?

- Will equity holders be required to provide guarantees for third-party finance?

- Will there be pre-emptive rights relating to new issues of shares?

- What happens if a shareholder fails to contribute?

7 Transfer of Shares

- Will there be restrictions on transfers of shares?

- Restrictions on equity holders encumbering their shares?

- Unanimous decision to transfer shares to a third party?

- Pre-emptive rights?

- A requirement for a new shareholder to be bound by the shareholders agreement?

- How will the sale shares be valued?

8 General Exit Strategies

- Some exit strategies include:

    › Buyouts between equity holders. For example, options may be granted to require any or a shareholder to sell out or an option in favour of shareholder to require other shareholders to buy them out in certain specified situations.

    › Operation of pre-emptive rights or rights of first refusal.

    › 'Drag-along' or 'tag-along' rights are also common.

9 Events of Default

- What happens if there is a material breach of the equity holders' agreement? Should the equity holder be forced to sell its shares? For example:
  - › an insolvency event occurs in relation to a shareholder (for example, receiver appointed, winding-up application, etc.)
  - › an equity holder sells its shares in breach of the equity holders' agreement
  - › there is a change in control of an equity holder.

10 Solutions for Deadlocks and Other Disputes

- What happens if a dispute or deadlock occurs between the equity holders? Some solutions include:
  - › The appointment of a mediator.
  - › The forced sale and purchase of shares between the equity holders. For example, 'shot-gun' provisions where one party can name a price at which it will sell and the other party has the right to buy at that price or to require the first party to buy it out at the price at which it is prepared to sell.
  - › Will there be provisions such as mechanisms to ensure completion? For example, power of attorney granted to purchaser equity holders or authorising the Company to register share transfers.
  - › A process to wind up the Company.

11 Management of the Company/Trustee Company

- What will be the management structure? For example:
  - › positions, titles and responsibilities
  - › bank signing authorities
  - › conduct of business
  - › who and how will day-to-day decisions be made
  - › consequences of death, incapacity and sickness?
- Leave provisions.

12 Records and Provisions of Information

- What records will the Company be required to prepare? And who should be provided access? For example:

    › Will periodic reports be prepared?

    › How will records be maintained?

    › How will shareholders access records?

APPENDIX C

RECORD-KEEPING REQUIREMENTS FOR ALL BUSINESS AREAS

The following table shows the legislation relating to document retention and destruction in different business areas. The information provided in the table is current as at April 2018.

Source	Relevant documents	Relevant section	Retention time
Income Tax Assessment Act (1936) (Cth)	Documents relevant to income and expenditure *Readily accessible and convertible into writing in English*	s262A	**5 years** after records were prepared or obtained, or after the completion of the transactions or acts to which the records relate, whichever is the later
Corporations Act (2001) (Cth)	Written financial records that: • correctly record and explain the business's transactions, financial position and performance; and • would make true and fair financial statements that are able to be prepared and audited.	s9 s286(1)(2) s287 s288 s289	**7 years** after the transactions covered by the records are completed
	Books containing the minutes or proceedings of any general meeting or of a meeting of the directors.	s251A s1101C	**5 years** after the last entry in the register; but preferably indefinitely or 7 years in addition to the life of the organisation
	Registers (of members, charges and option-holders)	s169 s168 s1101C s170	**5 years** after the last entry in the register
Fair Work Act 2009 (Cth)	Records of employees *In a legible form in the English language and readily accessible to an inspector.*	s535	**7 years** after termination of employment
Occupational Health and Safety Act 2004 (Vic)	Record of notifiable incidents	s38	**7 years**
Australian Charities and Not for Profit Commission Act 2012 (Cth)	Operational records	Part 3-2 s55-5	**7 years** but preferably 7 years in addition to the life of the organisation

Source	Relevant documents	Relevant section	Retention time
Anti-Money Laundering and Counter Financing Act 2006 (Cth)	Retain a copy of these records or an extract of the records showing the prescribed information (e.g. electronic storage of information).	Part 10 s107(2)	**7 years** after the making of the record
Financial Transaction Reports Act (1988) (Cth)	Cash dealers are to keep information obtained in the course of obtaining account information or signatory information.	s23(1)	**7 years** after the day on which the relevant account is closed
	Where a document is required to be released by law, a complete copy of it must be kept.	s23(7)	**7 year** period has ended or the document is returned, whichever occurs first
	A register of documents released	s23(5)	Keep indefinitely
	Any account or signatory information. In a way that can be audited (this includes reasonably accessible electronic form).	s23(1)	**7 years** after the day on which the relevant account is closed
	Financial institutions are to maintain a register for entering transactions and classes of transactions which are exempt significant cash transactions.	s12 s13	Keep indefinitely
Patents Act 1990 (Cth)	Standard Patents		**20 years** but good practice to keep for the duration that the IP right exists
Trade Marks Act 1995 (Cth)	Trademarks		**10 years** from the filing date of initial registration but good practice to keep for the duration that the IP right exists
Copyright Act 1968 (Cth)	Copyright		**70 years** after the end of the year of the creator's death but good practice to keep for the duration that the IP right exists

Source	Relevant documents	Relevant section	Retention time
Privacy Act 1988 (Cth)	Private sector organisations that are required to comply with the Privacy Act must take reasonable steps to destroy or permanently de-identify **personal information** if it is no longer needed for any purpose for which the information may be used or disclosed under the *Privacy Act.*	NPP 4.2 (to 12 March 2014)	When the personal information is no longer needed for any purpose for which it may be used or disclosed under the *Privacy Act.*
		APP 11.2 (after 12 March 2014)	
Health Practitioner Regulation (New South Wales) Regulation 2010; Health Records and Information Privacy Act (NSW) 2002; s25 *Health Records Act (Vic) 2001; s4.2* *Health Records (Privacy and Access) Act (ACT) 1997* Note: Tasmania, Qld and WA have no statutory period; however, MDA National considers these requirements to be appropriate in all Australian contexts.	Medical records – **Private practice only**	s10 s25 s4.2 Schedule 1	**7 years** from the date of the last entry if the patient was at least 18 at the time of the entry. If the patient was younger than 18 years at the date of the last entry, the record must be kept until the patient attains (or would have attained) 25 years. *From a medico-legal perspective, medical records should be kept until such time as there is little or no risk of litigation arising from the patient's treatment. This will depend upon the statutory limitation period within the relevant jurisdiction, and any applicable state or territory legislation governing medical records. Medical records for a patient who has a current claim for damages or who is subject to a Guardianship or other court or tribunal order should also be kept indefinitely, or until seven years after the patient's death. – MDA National*

Note: This table has a private sector focus and, therefore, does not address special record-retention issues particular to the public sector. It is intended only as a high-level aid to identifying relevant regimes and does not constitute legal advice. Public sector health providers in particular should seek specialised advised within their jurisdiction.

ABOUT YOU LEGAL

At You Legal, we provide the following:

- *Contracting and commercial advice:* We have a comprehensive understanding of commercial and business sensitivities. We regularly provide strategic and risk management advice, draft and review contracts and agreements.

- *Legislative and regulatory advice compliance:* You Legal lawyers are across all legislation and regulatory requirements that apply to our clients. We regularly write and share blogs relevant for our clients, and provide personalised advice to our clients as required.

- *Data protection and privacy advice:* Data protection and privacy have become prevalent issues in this digital age. You Legal's team are across all developments in Privacy, Freedom of Information and confidentiality.

- *Corporate:* You Legal advises on all aspects of corporate governance. You Legal prepares Shareholder's Agreements, assists in drafting Director's and Shareholder's Resolutions and provides Corporations Act advice to clients on a regular basis.

- *Employment:* You Legal's clients also rely on us for advice on all aspects of employment, from negotiating and drafting employment contracts, to workplace investigations and assistance with termination and suspension of employment arrangements. The team focuses on ensuring that all solutions provided to our clients are practical. You Legal's team understands that our clients need more than just a legal answer in order to achieve their overall goals.

- *HealthTech:* You Legal works with health sector entrepreneurs in developing novel ways of delivering health services by technology-based solutions. As the health sector is highly regulated, our clients depend on us for practical advice in navigating those complex laws and regulations. We have advised app developers, start-ups and established businesses about the privacy law obligations which apply to them, the obligations of health practitioners and the protection of intellectual property.

Go to youlegal.com.au for more information.